HOME AT LAST!

Steve & Audrey Eckert
RD 3 Box 153
Jackson, NJ 08527

HOME AT LAST!

WALTON J. BROWN

Review and Herald Publishing Association
Washington, DC 20039-0555
Hagerstown, MD 21740

Copyright © 1983 by the
Review and Herald Publishing Association

Edited by Bobbie Jane Van Dolson
Cover designed by Howard Bullard

Library of Congress Cataloging in Publication Data
Brown, Walton John.
   Home at last!

  1. Future life. 2. Heaven. 3. Eschatology. I. Title.
BT902.B76   1983   236'.2   83-11147

ISBN 0-8280-0200-2

Printed in U.S.A.

Contents

Preface—Speculation. Imagination. Reality.	7
The Death Sentence	11
Deliverance	17
One Week to Heaven	23
The Capital City	36
The First Thousand Years	44
Changing Concepts	52
The Last Battle	56
The New Earth	65
We, the People	72
Always Busy	75
Worship	83
On Becoming a Citizen	88

Preface

Speculation. Imagination. Reality.

For many centuries—even millenniums—Christians have looked forward with eager anticipation to the day when Jesus would return to fulfill His promise: "In my Father's house are many mansions. . . . I go to prepare a place for you. . . . I will come again, and receive you unto myself; that where I am, there ye may be also."[1]

Paul indicated that he was "looking for that blessed hope, and the glorious appearing of the great God and our Saviour Jesus Christ."[2]

In our own day we sing: "Come let us sing of homeland, Down by the crystal sea; Wonderful land where Jesus Buildeth a mansion for me."[3]

As Christians, we like to think of heaven and the new earth. We like to dream of it. We try to imagine what it will be like. At times we may let our fancies wander too far astray and go beyond the limits that God has set. Definite warnings have been given by Ellen White against this: "Spiritual fables are taking many captive. . . . To all who are indulging these unholy fancies, I would say, Stop; . . . stop right where you are. You are on forbidden ground."[4] "We need not enter into speculation regarding our future state."[5]

These warnings are given to discourage conjectures for which there is no divine revelation. "The secret things belong unto the Lord our God; but those things which are revealed belong unto us and to our children for ever."[6] "Christ withheld no truths essential to our salvation. Those things that are revealed are for us and our children, but we are not to allow our imagination to frame doctrines concerning things not revealed."[7] "Upon subjects not revealed, and having nought to do with our salvation, silence is eloquence."[8]

Christians "should not spend time speculating as to what conditions will prevail in the new earth. It is presumption to indulge

HOME AT LAST!

in suppositions and theories regarding matters that the Lord has not revealed! He has made every provision for our happiness in the future life, and we are not to speculate regarding His plans for us. Neither are we to measure the conditions of the future life by the conditions of this life."[9]

Why are we counseled to be careful in this matter? Because the "unfoldings of Jesus in reference to heavenly things are of a character that only the spiritual mind can appreciate. The imagination may summon its utmost powers in order to picture the glories of heaven, but 'eye hath not seen, nor ear heard, neither have entered into the heart of man, the things which God hath prepared for them that love him.' . . . Only by the spiritual vision can we discern heavenly things. Our human powers would be extinguished by the inexpressible glory of the angels of light."[10]

On the other hand, we are to avoid the opposite extreme. "A fear of making the future inheritance seem too material has led many to spiritualize away the very truths which lead us to look upon it as our home. Christ assured His disciples that He went to prepare mansions for them in the Father's house. Those who accept the teachings of God's word will not be wholly ignorant concerning the heavenly abode."[11]

"Satan has worked continually to eclipse the glories of the future world and to attract the whole attention to the things of this life. He has striven to arrange matters that our thought, our anxiety, our labor might be so fully employed in temporal things that we should not see or realize the value of eternal realities."[12]

For this reason Ellen White suggests that "these visions of future glory, scenes pictured by the hand of God, should be dear to His children. . . . We need to keep ever before us this vision of things unseen. It is thus that we shall be able to set a right value on the things of eternity and the things of time. It is this that will give us power to influence others for the higher life."[13]

"We may have a vision of the future, the blessedness of heaven. In the Bible are revealed visions of the future glory, scenes pictured in the hand of God, and these are dear to His church. By faith we may stand on the threshold of the eternal city, and hear the gracious welcome to those who in this life cooperate with Christ, regarding it as an honor to suffer for His sake."[14] "Work, oh, work, keeping

SPECULATION. IMAGINATION. REALITY.

eternity in view!" [15]

A legitimate use of the imagination is encouraged: "Let your imagination take hold upon things unseen. Let your thoughts be carried away to the evidences of the great love of God for you." [16] "Let your imagination picture the home of the saved, and remember that it will be more glorious than your brightest imagination can portray." [17]

In doing this, however, it must always be emphasized that "in thinking of heaven, we may put our imagination to the utmost stretch and think the loftiest thoughts that we are capable of thinking, and our minds will grow weary in the effort to comprehend the breadth and depth and height of the subject. It is impossible for our minds to take in the great themes of eternity. It is impossible for us even to make an effort to understand these things without the effort affecting our whole character for good and having an uplifting influence on our minds." [18]

"Human language is inadequate to describe the reward of the righteous. It will be known only to those who behold it." [19]

It is on this basis that we are launching forth on a description of heaven and the new earth as far as we understand that it has been revealed to us in the Holy Scriptures and in the writings of Ellen White. This description will be made as if earth's history had ended and several of us, with our loved ones and friends, have been redeemed by the blood of Jesus, and are describing what we see and are enjoying.

Up to a certain point, in order to tie the story together, we will let our imagination have play, but only as it connects revealed facts. Sources for ideas expressed will be found in the footnote references at the close of each chapter. Actual words found in these sources may be used, although, in general, quotation marks may be omitted, since at times parts of different quotations have been put together in order to give a more detailed and complete description, and the use of quotation marks could be misleading. At other times tenses have been changed.

I wish to express my profound appreciation to Elder Donald E. Mansell, of the Ellen G. White Estate, who kindly read this manuscript, made corrections and changes, and gave valuable recommendations for its improvement. I also wish to thank Elder Melvin W. Sickler, and my wife, Doreen, who read the manuscript

HOME AT LAST!

and offered constructive suggestions.

So let us begin the story with the last scenes in earth's present history, seeing the fulfillment of the blessed hope, and then travel heavenward, reaching HOME AT LAST! May the reader enjoy this book as much as I have enjoyed writing it!

Walton J. Brown

References

[1] John 14:2, 3.
[2] Titus 2:13.
[3] Henry de Fluiter, copyright 1918.
[4] *Medical Ministry*, p. 101.
[5] *Selected Messages*, book 1, p. 173.
[6] Deut. 29:29.
[7] *Medical Ministry*, p. 100.
[8] *Selected Messages*, book 2, pp. 25, 26.
[9] *Gospel Workers*, p. 314.
[10] I Cor. 2:9; *In Heavenly Places*, p. 366.
[11] *The Great Controversy*, pp. 674, 675.
[12] *The Adventist Home*, pp. 404, 405.
[13] *Child Guidance*, p. 568.
[14] *The Acts of the Apostles*, pp. 601, 602.
[15] *Testimonies*, vol. 9, p. 47.
[16] *Ibid.*, vol. 8, p. 125.
[17] *Steps to Christ*, p. 86.
[18] *In Heavenly Places*, p. 368.
[19] *The Story of Redemption*, pp. 430, 431.

Chapter One

The Death Sentence

The past few months had been difficult ones. A few of us had retired to homes not far from a large city, owing to the fact that some of our relatives and friends lived in that general area. We enjoyed attending the churches in that place, and participated in their activities. In some cases, wives continued to work for church organizations and in other places. Some of us did writing and at times even traveled in the fulfillment of tasks assigned by departments of the church we had worked for prior to retiring.

But then the situation changed. Turmoil throughout the world increased. The financial structure, affected by galloping inflation, deteriorated. Nations became more and more angry with one another, and as events took a downward turn, and the earth itself seemed to be changing for the worse, the words of Jesus, spoken almost two thousands years before, were fulfilled: "Men's hearts failing them for fear, and for looking after those things which are coming on the earth: for the powers of heaven shall be shaken."[1]

Apostasy and corruption reached such proportions that God finally withdrew His protecting power, and Satan, taking advantage of this, moved in with still more terrible calamities. In their desperation, people looked to God, trusting that He might save them, saying, "Come ye, and let us go to the mountain of the Lord, to the house of the God of Jacob; and he will teach us of his ways, and we will walk in his paths. . . . O house of Jacob, come ye, and let us walk in the light of the Lord."[2] But, like Cain of old, most insisted on worshiping God in their own way, following human traditions and not divine revelation. "Their land also is full of idols; they worship the work of their own hands, that which their own fingers have made."[3]

In the United States, various spiritual programs were promoted.

HOME AT LAST!

Religious organizations put more and more stress on observing Sunday, the first day of the week. They claimed that the calamities were a divine manifestation of displeasure resulting from Sunday desecration, and the movement for passing a national Sunday law gained momentum. Seventh-day Adventists countered by warning that the disasters were not the result of Sunday violation, but because of a general turning away from God. Nevertheless, a Sunday law was enacted. Discussions concerning the passage of this law had been extensive, and everyone had the opportunity to make a definite conscious decision for or against God's commands. Many chose to obey the commandments, for the time of probation was still open; but the majority turned away.[4]

The passage of the Sunday law in the United States had been to us a warning to leave the larger cities, preparatory to leaving the smaller towns to seek secluded dwelling places in the mountains.[5] Many heeded this warning and moved to rural communities.

Calamities continued, however, and it was around this time that the ark of the covenant, hidden in a cave by the righteous when Nebuchadnezzar had conquered Jerusalem more than twenty-five hundred years before and hidden since that time, was discovered. In it were the Ten Commandments just as they had been engraved by the finger of God on Mount Sinai.[6] This discovery focused attention on the seventh-day Sabbath, and for a time it appeared that the pendulum was swinging in favor of those who had been faithful in its observance.[7]

It was now that the crowning act in the great drama of deception took place. There had been others, but this was a strong, almost overmastering delusion. Satan impersonated Christ and appeared in different parts of the world, revealing himself as a majestic being of dazzling brightness. Shouts of triumph rang out, "Christ has come! Christ has come!" People prostrated themselves in adoration before the deceiver, and he lifted up his hands and pronounced blessings on them. His voice was soft and subdued, yet full of melody. In gentle, compassionate tones he repeated some of the same truths that Jesus had spoken.

In his assumed character of Christ, Satan declared that he had changed the observance of Sabbath to Sunday, and commanded all to hallow the day that he had blessed. He declared that those of us who

THE DEATH SENTENCE

persisted in keeping holy the seventh day were blaspheming his name and were offending God, and that the calamities would not cease as long as the Sunday sabbath was being violated. He added that those who presented the claims of the fourth commandment, thus destroying reverence for Sunday, were troublers of the people, preventing their restoration to divine favor and temporal prosperity.[8]

In response, the United States intensified its support of the Sunday law, and punished Sabbathkeepers, who were now accused of being enemies of religion. Persecution broke out with unprecedented fury. Various methods were employed to try to break down the will of the faithful, beginning with bribes, then threats, the abridgment of civil liberties, a boycott, and finally, after a time, the ultimate penalty—death.[9]

The situation became intolerable, and we were obliged to leave our comfortable homes, with all our "things" in them. With friends from several of the city churches, we fled, heading in our cars to the mountains a short distance away.[10] We knew that throughout the nation, others were doing the same. Some were being imprisoned, and others were being martyred. But many of us did make our escape.

Having done Satan's bidding in passing the law against the Sabbath, the United States seemed to find a temporary respite from disasters.[11] As other nations saw that the situation in America had apparently leveled off somewhat, they decided to follow its example of Sunday legislation. One after another they began to pass their own Sunday laws.[12] Because of this increased pressure, many members of the church abandoned their faith and became our bitterest enemies.[13] But the church, purified of doubtful elements, and under the influence of the latter rain, gave God's message, the loud cry, with renewed vigor—"Come out of her, my people."[14]

Finally, the nations of the world united in passing a universal law against the Sabbath. Soon after this Jesus stepped out of the Most Holy Place in heaven. The time of mercy ended. The period of probation for man ceased. At the same time there was a worldwide temporary decrease in calamities, and for a while people again took up their regular activities of planting, building, and carrying on business, not realizing that the final decision had been made, not knowing of the disaster that was about to strike. This decisive hour had come as a thief in the night.[15]

HOME AT LAST!

Those of us living in the Northern Hemisphere, where the major portion of the world's population was concentrated, were fortunate in the time of our flight, for it took place in the springtime, reminding us of the prayer that Jesus, long ago, had suggested to those who would flee from Jerusalem: "Pray ye that your flight be not in the winter, neither on the sabbath day." [16] Realizing that every earthly support would be cut off, we had not taken much with us when we left our homes—just a change of clothes, our Bibles, a few cherished Spirit of Prophecy books, a small quantity of food, and a few other necessities. It was not cold, and soon the berry bushes would begin to yield their fruit, providing something to eat when the little that we had taken along was consumed.

We drove our cars as far as possible, abandoning them where the road narrowed to a country path. We were not forsaken, however, for from this time onward we were under the care of angels, who had been instructed by Jesus to protect and help us. Our heavenly guides led us through brush, forests, and clefts of mountains. Finally, in a solitary place, we discovered some caves and covered hollows where we could hide and protect ourselves from the elements. We were told that there we would be safe. Isaiah, centuries before, had prophesied our situation: "His place of defence shall be the munitions of rocks; bread shall be given him; his waters shall be sure." [17] Recalling these words, we were comforted.

Still, during the following weeks, our suffering was intense—physical, because we had only minimal food and were exposed to heat and cold; and mental, because Satan constantly insinuated that we were lost, that we had unconfessed sins that had not been canceled by the blood of Jesus. Some who had come out with us, and seemed to be God's children, openly confessed that they had unforgiven sins, and left our group. This caused us much distress, making us wonder whether there was something in our own lives that would cause us to abandon hope. Those were days of anguish, the time that the Bible had described as "Jacob's trouble." [18]

Soon after the close of probation the plagues began to fall. The wicked were surprised when the effects of the first plague were felt, and infuriated when the second came. The afflictions were not universal, but where they fell they were the most terrible scourges that had ever been known to mortals. [19] The appearance of the third

THE DEATH SENTENCE

plague, coupled with the effects of the first two, provoked still greater hatred against us, and a universal movement for the destruction of God's people was organized. A death decree was enacted, and the exact day and hour was set to strike the decisive blow that would utterly silence the voice of dissent and reproof.[20]

Some enemies, however, anticipated the decree, and tried to kill us before the time specified. But none could pass the mighty angelic guardians stationed about us. Some of our number had been assailed as they fled from the cities and villages, but the swords raised against them broke and fell as powerless as straws. In other cases, guns refused to fire! In still other situations, God's people were defended by angels in the form of men of war.[21]

In spite of all that was taking place, we felt ourselves most fortunate, for while the world at large was dying of hunger, heat, and pestilence, angels protected us and continued to supply us with necessary food and water.[22] Those who were hunting us eventually discovered our abandoned cars, and inspired by evil angels, they soon had a good idea where we might be found. Nevertheless, they were kept from locating us, for we were protected by divine power.[23]

As week followed week we were comforted by close companionship and communion with our friends. We read together, prayed together, and talked of the deliverance that we knew was sure to come. We shared our Bibles, books, and periodicals, and encouraged one another as we read together.

Several of us had brought along solar-powered battery radios, in order to listen to the news. The situation was deteriorating swiftly, and hatred of those who were true followers of God, who refused to go the way of the majority, was becoming more intense day by day. We heard of wars that broke out here and there throughout the world. We heard of the death sentence that had been passed on us. Nevertheless, our confidence in God remained unshaken, for we remembered His promises and trusted in them.[24]

Persecution against God's people escalated into the worst in all history. We were convinced that this was a part of the final battle of Armageddon, with the powers of evil lined up against Providence itself. We were filled with confidence as we remembered that through Ellen White, God had said, "The Captain of the Lord's host will stand at the head of the angels of heaven to direct the battle."[25]

HOME AT LAST!

References

[1] Luke 21:26.
[2] Isa. 2:3-5.
[3] Verse 8.
[4] *Testimonies*, vol. 5, pp. 462, 463.
[5] *Ibid.*, pp. 464, 465.
[6] *Prophets and Kings*, p. 453; *The SDA Bible Commentary*, Ellen G. White Comments, on Ex. 31:18, p. 1109; Ellen G. White Comments, on Rev. 11:19, p. 972.
[7] *General Conference Bulletin*, 1895, p. 423; cf. *General Conference Bulletin*, 1893, p. 519.
[8] *Testimonies to Ministers*, p. 62; *The Great Controversy*, pp. 590, 624.
[9] Rev. 13:17; *Testimonies to Ministers*, p. 473; *The Great Controversy*, p. 592; *Selected Messages*, book 2, p. 380.
[10] *The Great Controversy*, pp. 613-615, 626.
[11] *Testimonies*, vol. 1, p. 268.
[12] *Ibid.*, vol. 6, p. 18.
[13] *The SDA Bible Commentary*, Ellen G. White Comments, on Acts 20:30, p. 1065.
[14] Rev. 18:1, 4.
[15] I Thess. 5:2; *Maranatha*, p. 264; Ellen G. White, in *Review and Herald*, Nov. 9, 1905.
[16] Matt. 24:20.
[17] Isa. 33:16; *Maranatha*, p. 270; *The Desire of Ages*, pp. 121, 122; Manuscript 53, 1905.
[18] Jer. 30:7; *Early Writings*, pp. 36, 37; *The Great Controversy*, p. 619.
[19] *The Great Controversy*, pp. 628, 629.
[20] *Ibid.*, p. 635; *Testimonies*, vol. 1, p. 204.
[21] *The Great Controversy*, p. 631.
[22] *Ibid.*, pp. 629, 634; *Early Writings*, p. 282; *Maranatha*, p. 270.
[23] *Prophets and Kings*, p. 513; *Historical Sketches*, p. 158; *Maranatha*, p. 270.
[24] *The Great Controversy*, pp. 619, 626, 629, 633.
[25] Dan. 12:1; *Maranatha*, pp. 290, 297; *The SDA Bible Commentary*, Ellen G. White Comments, on Rev. 16:13-16, pp. 982, 983.

Chapter Two

Deliverance

The date for our destruction arrived. At midnight we were to be killed, and it was in this hour of extremity, in accordance with His promise, that God interposed for the deliverance of His people. At this time the effect of the fifth plague was felt, and a dense blackness, deeper than the darkness of the night, fell upon the earth.[1] Then a rainbow, shining with glory from the throne of God, spanned the heavens. Bands of attackers that had been approaching to administer the death sentence stopped in wonderment. Their mocking cries died away as with fear in their faces they looked upon that glorious bow.

Those of us who were hiding in the secret places of the earth had anticipated this. At the entrance of our retreats, we had set watchers to tell us when the first signs of deliverance appeared. Now we left our dens and caves and stood outside. The rainbow appeared to encircle us as well as other like groups that we could see in the distance, and we knew that the same thing was happening to similar faithful bands all over the world.

Shortly afterward the rainbow faded away and the sun came out, shining in full strength. Signs and wonders followed in quick succession. The seventh angel now poured out his vial into the air, and "there were voices, and thunders, and lightnings; and there was a great earthquake, such as was not since men were upon the earth, so mighty an earthquake, and so great. . . . And there fell upon men a great hail out of heaven: . . . and men blasphemed God because of the plague of the hail; for the plague thereof was exceeding great."[2]

Another event now took place that, because of our knowledge of the Word of God, we had anticipated. Certain individuals were resurrected to see the second coming of the Lord. Daniel's prophecy,

HOME AT LAST!

given two and one-half millenniums before, was now fulfilled. "And many of them that sleep in the dust of the earth shall awake, some to everlasting life, and some to shame and everlasting contempt."[3] Ellen White, seeing this scene in vision, had said, "All who have died in the faith of the third angel's message come forth from the tomb glorified, to hear God's covenant of peace with those who have kept His law."[4]

We knew that our loved ones who had died in Jesus were now alive. We felt sure that they could see exactly what we were seeing, and that with us were exclaiming, "Lo, this is our God; we have waited for him, and he will save us: this is the Lord, we have waited for him, we will be glad and rejoice in his salvation."[5]

In this same resurrection others of a far different nature had also arisen: "They also which pierced him: and all kindreds of the earth shall wail because of him."[6] "Those that mocked and derided Christ's dying agonies, and the most violent opposers of His truth and His people, are raised to behold Him in His glory, and to see the honor placed upon the loyal and obedient." "Those who derided His claim to be the Son of God are speechless now. There is the haughty Herod who jeered at His royal title and bade the mocking soldiers crown Him king. There are the very men who with impious hands placed upon His form the purple robe, upon His sacred brow the thorny crown, and in His unresisting hand the mimic scepter, and bowed before Him in blasphemous mockery. The men who smote and spit upon the Prince of life now turn from His piercing gaze. . . . Those who drove the nails through His hands and feet, the soldier who pierced His side, behold these marks with terror and remorse." The priests and rulers who had led out in the attack on Him now recall the events of Calvary.[7]

The final destructive earthquake was making its effects felt. In fear, our assailants sought to escape from the judgments of God, which were now manifest to all. Some had hurried past us as we emerged from our hiding places. Now the wicked, with the natural instinct of self-preservation, "hid themselves in the dens and in the rocks of the mountains," but at the same time, in fear, "said to the mountains and rocks, Fall on us, and hide us from the face of him that sitteth on the throne . . . for the great day of his wrath is come; and who shall be able to stand?"[8]

As our persecutors entered the caves, in many cases the same ones

DELIVERANCE

that we had left just a short while before, they found the books and periodicals that we had left inside. As some looked at these they began to accuse one another, realizing that they had been misled and were eternally lost. Among those who fled were religious leaders who had organized the attacks against us. Now they were being denounced in scathing words, "It was you who made light of the truth. It was you who voiced the false doctrines when I was convicted that these Seventh-day Adventists had the truth. The blood of our souls is upon your priestly garments. . . . Now will you pay the ransom for my soul? . . . What shall we do who listened to your garbling of the Scriptures?" [9]

The wicked who had remained in the open and were not destroyed continued to look in terror and amazement upon the scene. Streams ceased to flow. Dark, heavy clouds came up and clashed against one another.

Then through a break in the clouds, a star beamed with a brilliancy four times the darkness. In hope and joy we sang out, "'God is our refuge and strength, a very present help in trouble. Therefore will not we fear, though the earth be removed, and though the mountains be carried into the midst of the sea; though the waters thereof roar and be troubled, though the mountains shake with the swelling thereof.'" [10]

While these words were ascending to God, the clouds were swept back, and there appeared a hand holding two tables of stone folded together. It was God's holy law revealed again to man as the rule of judgment. The hand opened the tables, and there were seen the precepts of the decalogue, traced as with a pen of fire. The words were so plain that all could read them. They were an exact transcription of the law given to Moses, the same law that had been found before the close of probation. [11] The wicked were filled with horror and despair as they realized their guilt, knowing that they had trampled on God's holy requirements. With awful distinctness they saw that they were without excuse. They had chosen to serve the wrong master. [12]

Out of the glory that all were beholding came the voice of God like the sound of many waters, delivering the everlasting covenant. Our faces were lighted up with His glory, and the wicked could not look upon us. When the blessing was pronounced on those who had honored God by keeping His Sabbath holy, we let loose a mighty

HOME AT LAST!

shout of victory.[13]

Not long afterward, some of our group who had been gazing at the heavens excitedly called out, "Look! Look! Look over there!" When we asked, "Where?" they pointed out a small black cloud, about half the size of a man's hand.[14] In solemn silence we gazed upon it. As it grew larger and drew nearer the earth, the cloud's darkness faded completely away, and it became one large burst of indescribable glory. At the same time we heard strains of beautiful music, anthems of celestial melody, growing in volume as Jesus and His angels neared the earth.[15]

In a short time the bright cloud drew very close to earth and covered every bit of the sky from horizon to horizon. While at first we had not been able to distinguish individual figures, these soon became recognizable. We could see angels moving about and preparing for what we knew would be one of the greatest events of history. From previous knowledge we knew that there were at least a hundred million of these heavenly beings.[16] Their exact number, of course, could not be calculated by us, nor did we know the number of the redeemed. We knew that the angels were at least twice as numerous as the saved of earth, since the latter were taking the place of the third part of angels who had been cast out of heaven with Lucifer.[17]

Finally, we saw the central Figure in all of His glory, Jesus Himself, the Son of God. He was now seen in His own glory as well as the glory of His Father and that of the angels. He was clad in the robe of the whitest light that He had worn from the days of eternity. His hair was white and curly and lay on His shoulders. His feet had the appearance of fire. In His right hand there was a sharp sickle, and in His left a silver trumpet. His eyes were as a flame of fire. On His head He wore a plural crown of glory, actually a crown within a crown. Words completely fail to describe this tremendous scene.[18]

Now another phase of the judgment took place in the presence of all the worlds, the public manifestation of who would be saved and who would be lost.[19]

At this time we heard the sound of the trumpet ringing loud and clear over hills and dales and, we were sure, over the entire earth. At the same time millions of angels left the heavenly cloud and went out in every direction—north, south, east, and west. They departed with great joy, for they were the angels who had accompanied certain

DELIVERANCE

individuals throughout life and had seen these people laid to rest to await the call of their Lord. Now these heavenly guardians would greet the risen ones as soon as Jesus called them from their graves.

In the silence that followed the sounding of the trumpet, Jesus, now near the earth, called out in a loud voice that was heard by all, even by those sleeping in the tombs, "Awake! Awake! ye that sleep in the dust, and arise." At the same time the earth was again shaken by a great earthquake, and graves were opened. The voice of Christ penetrated the tomb and pierced the ears of the sleeping saints, and all the righteous dead emerged.[20] All, from Adam on down, came out clothed in immortality. Their last thought had been of death and its pangs, of the grave and of the tomb, but now pain was gone and they arose in perfection, proclaiming, "O death, where is thy sting? O grave, where is thy victory?"[21]

As each person stepped from the grave he was greeted by his own angel, who, unseen, had been his guardian from his earliest moment. This angel had watched his steps and covered his head in the midst of peril, had been with him in the valley of the shadow of death and had marked his resting place, and now was there to meet him when the life-giving voice had sounded. Now these angels guided their newly resurrected friends on their way to meet the Lord in the air. The earth was ringing with the tread of the exceeding great army coming in from every nation, kindred, tongue, and people. As they moved away from the prison house of death all were clothed with immortal glory. As they marched upward a great cry of victory came from them, and we who watched the transformation of those closest to us joined them.[22]

While the resurrection was taking place, something was also happening to us. Since shortly after we had left the caves, changes had been taking place that affected both our attitudes and our appearance. Now, as we watched, in one moment, in the twinkling of an eye, we saw the great completion of this change. A wonderful physical transformation came over us, and we were clothed with immortality.

We now distinguished angel forms appearing beside us. Each was noble looking, and was clothed in glory. They presented themselves to us, saying that they were our guardian angels, who had accompanied us during the entire time we had lived on earth.[23]

Immediately afterward these angels spoke most welcome words:

HOME AT LAST!

"Follow us," they invited. "We are now going to lead you to meet your Lord and Saviour." As soon as they said this, our feet left the ground, and we slowly ascended. As more and more of the redeemed came from all over the earth, the group moving upward grew larger and larger, with the angels gradually forming columns on either side. As we rose higher and higher, an angelic choir struck up a song of victory. The angels in the two columns took up the strain and joined in the anthem, and then we, those who had been saved and were leaving the earth below, joined in. There was not an unharmonious note.[24] Oh, what music!

No wonder that we sang! This blessed hope, now being fulfilled, had accompanied us through life, and for many of us even into the grave. Now we could enjoy the fulfillment of it. We knew in whom we had believed. We had not run or labored in vain. The time of jubilee had begun when we would rest, when the land would rest. The promise of Jesus had been fulfilled. He had returned. He was receiving us unto Himself. Now we would be with Him forever. A rich, glorious reward was before us, the prize for which we had run. Now we would meet Jesus Himself, face to face![25]

References

[1] Rev. 16:10, 11.
[2] Verses 18-21; *The Great Controversy*, p. 636; *Maranatha*, p. 290.
[3] Dan. 12:2.
[4] *The Great Controversy*, p. 637; cf. *Early Writings*, p. 285.
[5] Isa. 25:9.
[6] Rev. 1:7.
[7] *The Great Controversy*, pp. 637, 643.
[8] Rev. 6:15-17.
[9] *Maranatha*, p. 290.
[10] Ps. 46:1-3.
[11] *The SDA Bible Commentary*, Ellen G. White Comments, on Ex. 31:18, p. 1109.
[12] *Ibid.*, *The Great Controversy*, pp. 639, 640, 435.
[13] *The Great Controversy*, p. 640.
[14] *Ibid.*
[15] *Ibid.*, pp. 640, 641.
[16] Rev. 5:11; 19:14; *The Great Controversy*, p. 641.
[17] Chap. 12:4; *Testimonies*, vol. 5, p. 291, 473; vol. 3, p. 115; Ellen G. White, in *Review and Herald*, May 29, 1900.
[18] *Early Writings*, p. 16; *Our High Calling*, p. 367; *Maranatha*, p. 292.
[19] *Maranatha*, p. 292.
[20] John 5:28, 29; Matt. 24:31; I Thess. 4:16; *Life Sketches*, p. 66; *Early Writings*, p. 16.
[21] I Cor. 15:55; *Sons and Daughters of God*, p. 359; *Early Writings*, pp. 16, 287; *The Great Controversy*, p. 645; *The Desire of Ages*, p. 606; *The SDA Bible Commentary*, Ellen G. White Comments, on I Cor. 15:51, p. 1093.
[22] *The Great Controversy*, p. 645; *Education*, pp. 305, 127.
[23] I Thess. 4:17; I Cor. 15:52; *Early Writings*, p. 287; *Education*, p. 305; *The Great Controversy*, pp. 638, 639.
[24] *Sons and Daughters of God*, p. 359.
[25] *In Heavenly Places*, p. 352; *Sons and Daughters of God*, p. 359.

Chapter Three

One Week to Heaven

On our way to meet Jesus, everyone rejoiced, including our guardian angels. As we rose higher in the air, our number increased as more and more, the resurrected and those who had been translated came together. Once in a while we saw people that we recognized and we would call out to them, "Alleluia!" but we did not delay, for we were so very eager to meet our loved ones. Some of us asked our guardian angels to guide us to where people from our hometowns were ascending. They agreed immediately and led toward different sections of the congregating hosts.

We slowed our pace to observe some heartwarming scenes. Babies who had just arisen from their dusty beds came forth, and their guardian angels guided them to their mothers' arms. The rapture of these women as they received their children and realized that now they would see them grow into perfect, everlasting adulthood was so evident that it thrilled our hearts. Other similar scenes were not mixed with the same joy, for there were those whose mothers were not among the redeemed. But such infants were not neglected. Their guardian angels received them and took personal care of them on the way to heaven.[1]

Our guardian angels led us as we threaded our way through the enormous multitudes that were ascending, and—then we saw them! There were our fathers and mothers and uncles and aunts. But how different they looked from when we had seen them the last time as we had laid them to rest! Then they had been old, wrinkled, and bent. Some had been very sick before death, and this had changed their appearance. Now they were young and strong. Their wrinkles were gone. All evidences of ill health and disease and old age had been wiped out, and their forms were symmetrical and perfect. All

HOME AT LAST!

blemishes and imperfections had been left in the grave! And as we rushed together with exclamations of joy, we had no trouble recognizing one another in our immortal beauty.[2]

They, in turn, were overjoyed at seeing us, and commented on our pleasant appearance. Some of our features had been changed, but our friends and loved ones knew us and said that we looked just the way we had when we were young, adding that we were even better looking.

As we continued on our way upward, our guardian angels explained that God had planned things so that personal identity was perfectly preserved in the resurrection and the transformation. The bodies of the redeemed were not composed of the same particles that had gone into the grave, but were now made up of much finer material. They had gone down to death as natural sinful bodies. Now they were raised as spiritual bodies, and were gifted with a higher nature than before, similar to that of Christ. In death the spirit, the character, but not a conscious entity, had returned to God and there had been preserved. At resurrection each person who had been resting in the grave had received back his own character and had also received the same individuality of features. Those who had been translated preserved their character and their features. Because of this we could recognize not only our loved ones but also our friends. In making a comparison, the angels explained this transformation as being similar to plants that grow from a sown kernel of grain.[3]

We were now nearing the point not far above the earth where Jesus sat on His throne, surrounded by a large number of angels. Our guardian angels had left us for a while to join one of the two columns of angels that were accompanying the multitude of saints, one column on each side. Now, forgetting all that was around us, we focused our attention on the scene before us. Our heads were uplifted, and the bright beams of the Sun of Righteousness shone upon us as we drew nearer the throne.[4] All fear of seeing Jesus, of seeing God the Father, face to face, was gone. Through divine aid we had formed perfect characters. Every sinful tendency, every imperfection, had been removed by the blood of the Saviour. The excellence and brightness of His glory, far exceeding the brightness of the sun in its meridian splendor, had been imparted to us. The moral beauty, the perfection of Jesus' character shining through us, was worth far more than this outward splendor. We now stood before our Saviour without fault, sharing the dignity and privileges of the angels.[5]

Jesus then spoke and welcomed His children to a new life, repeating the greeting that had been given by the guardian angels at the opened graves and to those of us who had been transformed from mortal to immortal beings. There He saw one who had looked with hope from his deathbed to the Saviour. Here was a former drunkard who in his longing to overcome his weakness had trusted in Christ to gain the victory.[6] As Jesus looked over the vast multitude, a look of satisfaction, visible to all of us, crossed His face. Both He and His Father were obviously content. As Jesus saw the result of His sacrifice, He beheld the recompense and was happy.[7] "And such is the value of the soul that the Father is satisfied with the price paid; and Christ Himself, beholding the fruits of His great sacrifice, is satisfied."[8]

We were now ready to begin our journey heavenward. Below, we could see the earth in devastation. Ruins and dead bodies were everywhere. Those who had not been destroyed by falling mountains, hail, or disease had been consumed by the brightness of the coming of the Lord.[9] This phase of the judgment scene, the first death, had taken place not only before our eyes, but in the presence of the inhabitants of the myriads of other worlds. The government of God had been vindicated, and His law stood forth as "holy, and just, and good." Every case had been decided, and sentence passed upon all. Sin had ceased to appear attractive, and was now seen in all its hideous magnitude.[10]

Now began the journey toward the open space in Orion and the heavenly capital beyond. We had already come to understand that speed was a relative thing. On earth, riding a horse had seemed swift compared to walking. Riding on a train had seemed fast compared to riding a horse. And some of us recalled traveling around the world on a jet, speeding through the air at almost six hundred miles an hour, and yet, as we had traveled, the plane had hardly seemed to be moving at all. Astronauts who journeyed to the moon at twenty-five thousand miles an hour had no sense of great speed. And so it was now. The immense cloud, with the multitude of redeemed together with the millions of accompanying angels, was now hastening toward Orion at what we calculated to be close to five light-years an hour.[11] And yet our cloudy chariot was so large that we were not aware of the speed or

HOME AT LAST!

even of any movement.

It took us a total of seven days to make the journey to the New Jerusalem.[12] This was much slower than when Jesus and His glorious companions had come down to the world. Then they had made the entire journey in a half day. It was thus that there was silence in heaven for seven and a half days, for heaven was emptied as the angels came down with Jesus to bring the children of God home.[13]

Ours was a living, glorious transport. Wings were on each side of this cloudy chariot, and beneath it were living wheels. As the chariot rolled upward the wheels would cry "Holy," and the living wings, as they moved, cried, "Holy," and then the retinue of angels all around cried, "Holy, holy, holy, Lord God Almighty." Then all of those that had been rescued from the world sang out, "Glory! Alleluia!" as the chariot continued its speedy flight to heaven.[14]

Not all of the time was spent in travel, for on the way we stopped to spend the first Sabbath with the heavenly hosts. It was a wonderful day as we sang, gave glory to God, and listened to Jesus as He spoke to us, telling a little of what He had in store for us. The thought occurred to us that this wonderful experience was giving those who had never kept a Sabbath on earth an opportunity to participate in the observance of at least one such day of rest before entering heaven. During the day we visited not only with our own individual guardian angels but also with others of the celestial beings.

We were not idle during the other six days of the journey. We moved back and forth on the vast expanse of the speeding cloud-chariot, talking with old friends, exchanging information with the loved ones from whom we had been separated, and enjoying the feeling of absolute freedom from fear. As we passed various constellations on the way to the celestial capital, we noticed with great interest and wondering eyes the modification in their shapes as our perspective of them swiftly changed.

As we moved about during those days, we observed the effects that sin had had upon the human race. On earth we had been of various heights, depending on the time we had lived during the world's six-thousand-year history. In the redeemed crowd we saw some who were double our height, and knew that these had made their decision in antediluvian days to be on God's side. My angel pointed out Adam, the father of our race. He was of lofty height and majestic form, in stature just a bit below the Son of God. He presented a marked contrast to the people of later generations, in this one respect showing the great degeneracy of the race. Nevertheless, size now made no difference. Where previously the human race had been mortal, corruptible, and defective, it was now perfect, beautiful, and immortal, possessed with the freshness and vigor of eternal youth.[15]

Among the most interesting conversations during the week-long journey were those with the angels, either privately or in groups. On one such occasion some of us were sitting with a number of angels, and were talking about some of the things that had happened on earth. First one angel and then another proceeded to explain some things in our life experiences that had perplexed us, and we began to realize more fully just what part these good friends of ours had played.

One angel recalled being present in a council hall watching a persecuted follower of Christ whose case apparently was lost. Taking human form, the angel had launched a fervent, successful appeal in the man's behalf. Another angel declared that he had done the same thing in another court of justice. Still others remembered instances when they had defeated purposes and evils that would have brought wrong and suffering to God's children. When we asked just how they had done this, whether they had exercised their powers unseen for the most part, they answered that they had been visible. The authorities had looked on them, and their ears had heard their pleas, but they had not realized that they were in the presence of angels of God.[16]

On other occasions our own guardian angels reminded us of some narrow escapes that we had had, and told us of efforts they had made to protect us.

Not all of the angels had been occupied in ministering to God's people on earth. Through the centuries, a good number of them had been working in heaven making crowns for the faithful—crowns, we were informed, that we would receive at the end of our journey. They had formed the crowns, setting in them beautiful gems in the form of stars that would reflect, with splendor, the light that radiates from the throne of God.[17] Still other angels had been busy at various tasks assigned them by the Godhead.

During these days, as we traveled to different places in the cloudy chariot, we became acquainted with or recognized more and more

HOME AT LAST!

people. Of course, we spent much time with our loved ones and with many of the friends with whom we had worked on earth, but now we made new friends, some of whom we had only read about in the Bible.

Adam, of course, was one of the most outstanding figures, and with him was his wife, Eve, the mother of our race.[18] It was evident that the shock of that first horrible disaster that had led to the loss of their second son was not yet forgotten as they walked around with Abel, the first human being to suffer death.[19] As the three of them moved among the multitude of Adam's descendants, they would at times stop while Adam and Eve presented one or another of their immediate children or grandchildren to Abel, who had never gotten to know any of them.

Righteous Enoch had greeted his ancestor Adam very soon after the resurrection, and told him of how he had been taken to heaven by God some 57 years after Adam's death. As a middle-aged man of 622 Adam had heard of Enoch's birth. He had known him as boy and man and had appreciated his sincerity and his love for the heavenly Father. When Adam was 687 years old, Enoch had brought his son Methuselah to receive a blessing from this man of God.[20] Three hundred years later, while still a young man, Enoch had become the first descendant of Adam to enter heaven's gates.[21]

Enoch was an interesting figure to behold. On his right arm he wore a glorious palm with the word "Victory" inscribed on each leaf. Around his head was a dazzling white wreath, composed of leaves, and in the middle of each leaf was written "Purity." Around this wreath were stones of various colors that shone brighter than the stars and cast a reflection upon the letters, magnifying them. On the back of Enoch's head was a bow that confined the wreath, and upon the bow was written "Holiness." Above the wreath was a crown that shone brighter than the sun.[22]

One day we saw Enoch, who lived in the capital city, in conversation with a man we had always admired and been eager to see. Moses, unlike Enoch, had passed under the dominion of death, but Christ Himself had called him from the grave to life, winning a dispute with Satan concerning his body.[23]

We saw Elijah, who, without seeing death, had traveled to heaven in a fiery chariot more than 2,800 years before.[24] When we first noticed him, he had his arm around Elisha, his earthly helper to

ONE WEEK TO HEAVEN

whom he had dropped his mantle as he was caught up into heaven.[25]

On another occasion, as we were strolling about, we saw a group of people surrounding a woman whose picture we had seen frequently and in whom we had believed as a messenger of the Lord. Her features were perfect now. There was no scar on her face, and she was in the full bloom of youth. She was Ellen Gould Harmon White,[26] and she stood next to her husband, James.[27] A child named Eva held her hand.[28] An old friend, Martha C. Hastings,[29] stood nearby listening closely to a lively conversation between the Whites and Elders Charles Fitch and Levi Stockman, who had befriended young Ellen at the beginning of her service for the Lord.[30] At another time we saw Ellen visiting an attractive women with several children and young people around her. We learned that she was Mrs. Angeline Stevens Andrews, wife of J. N. Andrews. With her was her daughter Mary and her other children.[31]

Another unforgettable sight was David standing arm in arm with Jonathan, the dear friend of his youth. Both were listening in rapt attention to Samuel, who had anointed David when he was but a lad.[32]

As we accompanied our guardian angels, they pointed out individuals in whom they thought we might be interested. These were also walking around and visiting friends—William Miller who, like Moses, had erred shortly before his death; the thief on the cross who had accepted Jesus when their earthly lives were about to end;[33] Noah, the faithful preacher of righteousness before the Flood; Abraham and his wife, Sarah, as they visited with their son, Isaac, and their grandson Jacob; Job, who in the depths of despair was still certain that he would be resurrected; and Peter and John, Jesus' intimate friends on earth.[34] Among others identified for us were loyal prophets who had testified for their Lord before the first coming of Jesus to earth, such men as Isaiah, Jeremiah, Habbakuk, Hosea, Ezekiel, Amos, Haggai, Micah, Zechariah, and Malachi.[35]

We were disappointed to discover that certain persons we had surely expected to see in heaven were not there. On the other hand, there were individuals there whom we had never thought to see. We had judged them by their outward appearance, as human beings were prone to do, but God had looked at their hearts and judged them by what they really were, and had saved them.[36]

Then our angels informed us that among the heathen were many

HOME AT LAST!

who had worshiped God ignorantly, to whom the light of truth had never been brought by human instrumentality, yet they were among this multitude of saved. Though ignorant of the written law of God, these earnest people had heard His voice speaking to them in nature, and had done the things that the law required. Their works were evidence that the Holy Spirit had touched their hearts, and they had been acknowledged by God as His children. How happy and how surprised they were to hear from the lips of their Saviour, "Inasmuch as ye have done it unto one of the least of these my brethren, ye have done it unto me."[37]

From time to time we met individuals who threw their arms around us and greeted us with special warmth as we stood near the great white throne. These persons told us that we had had a part in directing them to the uplifted Saviour. What wonderful conversations we had with them! One said, "I was a sinner without God and without hope in the world, and you came to me and drew my attention to the precious Saviour as my only hope." Others indicated that when we were missionaries in far-off lands we had come to them and helped them to walk in the narrow way. As we went from place to place we saw and overheard others speaking to some of our companions, expressing gratitude to them for having fed them when they were hungry, for having treated them as brethren, for having sympathized with them in their sorrow, and for having restored their bruised and wounded souls. What rejoicing there was as these redeemed ones met and greeted those who had had a part in saving them from the world, which was now so far behind.[38] With gladness unspeakable in our hearts we beheld those who, through the Holy Spirit, we had won for Christ. These in turn had gained others, and these still others, all brought into the haven of rest.[39]

And so the days passed as we rapidly approached the end of the journey. On the sixth day there was much bustle and activity, and all of us watched with keen interest. We were told that we were not far from the New Jerusalem, and that the Commander had given orders that a goodly number of angels speed on ahead to the city to make the final preparations for our arrival. Amid trumpet sounds and celestial singing, a large group of angels spread their wings, soared forth, and soon left us behind.

Toward the end of the next day, away in the distance, we caught our first glimpse of our destination. We saw a shining expanse that soon resolved itself into a large and beautiful city. It was God's capital, the New Jerusalem, the center of His universe.

Again we saw a demonstration of the organization and order that pervades all heavenly activities.[40] All of us, the redeemed, were now organized into a perfect square, with Jesus in the center seated on His uplifted throne. His majestic form and lovely countenance could be seen by all of us in the huge square, no matter how far away we were located.[41] In the process we were subdivided into various groups.

There was a planned order in our arrangement. Nearest the throne were those who had once been zealous workers for Satan, but who, as plucked from the burning, had followed their Saviour with deep, intense devotion.[42] Also close to the throne were the 144,000, who had been translated from the earth just one week before from among the living, and were counted as "the firstfruits unto God and to the Lamb." These were persons with no guile in their mouths. They had perfected Christian characters in the midst of falsehood and infidelity, and had honored the law of God when the so-called Christian world had declared it void. They had come through the tribulation such as never was, and had stood without an intercessor through the final outpouring of God's judgments. They had seen the earth wasted with famine and pestilence and by a broiling sun, and had suffered hunger and thirst.[43]

Together with this group were the millions of all ages who had been martyred for their faith. Most of these had gone down to the grave loaded with infamy, and had been judged by human courts as the vilest of criminals.[42]

And then, beyond these groups, stretched a great multitude, which no man could number, of all nations, and kindreds, and people, and tongues—millions and millions of them. These had come from hovels, from dungeons, from scaffolds, from mountains, from the caves of the earth, and from the caverns of the sea. On earth they had often been destitute, afflicted, and tormented. Now they stood before the throne in richer vestments than the most honored of the earth had ever worn. Henceforth they were to be ever with the Lord.

Among the millions that waited before the throne none ascribed salvation to himself. No one said anything of what he had done or suffered, but the burden of every song, the keynote of every anthem,

HOME AT LAST!

was "Salvation to our God, and unto the Lamb."[42]

We were now on the outskirts of the Holy City, close to the walls. We could distinguish angels as they were flying from one place to another on errands. And then from the city emerged a large number of these messengers of God, who flew toward the enormous square where we were waiting outside the city. They were carrying glorious golden crowns, shining harps, and palms. As they arrived where Jesus was sitting on His throne, Jesus called for the crowns, and the angels presented them to Him as He requested them. Then with His own right hand He placed the crowns on the heads of each one of us, crowns decked with diadems more glorious than any earthly monarch had ever worn. As we looked at our crowns later, we discovered that our new names were inscribed on them, as well as the words "Holiness to the Lord."

Special mention must be made of the reaction of parents when they saw the crowns, the robes, and the harps given to their children. It was with joy unutterable that they watched and realized that their children were saved. Various ones among the redeemed voiced special thanks to their mothers. As they received their crowns, they raised them in the sight of the assembled universe, and pointing to their mothers, said, "She made me all I am through the grace of God. Her instruction, her prayers, have been blessed to my eternal salvation."

After the ceremony of giving out the crowns had been completed, Jesus did the same with the harps. Finally, victor's palms were handed each one of us. Then, as the angelic choir gave the pitch, we all played our harps and sang.[44]

As we looked around the host of redeemed, we observed that the crowns were not all the same. Some were very bright, others not so bright. Some crowns appeared heavy with stars, while others had but few. Our guardian angels explained to us that the differences were based upon the attitudes of their bearers towards others while on earth. Those who received the most abundant reward were those who had mingled with their activity and zeal a gracious, tender pity for the poor, the orphan, the oppressed, and the afflicted. They were surprised to find that Christ had noticed every kind word spoken to the disheartened, and had taken account of the smallest gift that had been given for the relief of the poor and had cost the giver some self-denial. The crowns varied in their opulence, yet there was no sign of unhappiness among the owners. All of us were perfectly satisfied with our own crowns.[45]

Now the enormous congregation of redeemed and angels moved slowly toward the city on what appeared to be a sea of glass. Jesus left the center of the square; a path opened for Him through the crowd; and He passed through to the head of the large square of the ransomed. As we drew near the gates of the city, angels, both inside the city and surrounding us, touched their golden harps, and welcomed their King and His trophies of victory, those who had been washed and made white in His blood. It was a song of triumph that pealed forth, filling all of heaven. Christ had conquered.[46]

Now Jesus had reached one of the gates of the city. As antiphonal angelic choirs sang in response to each other, He laid hold of the gate and swung it back on its glittering hinges, and speaking in a voice that could be heard by all, bade the nations of redeemed, "You have washed your robes in My blood, stood stiffly for My truth, enter in." We accepted His invitation, feeling that we had a perfect right to do so, and slowly moved through the gate down a wide street of the city to a huge square in the center. On the way we saw rich glory everywhere, marvelous sights on which to feast the eye, but we did not linger. All of this we would see later. After arriving at the square, we and the angels stood quietly waiting for Jesus to speak.

Christ stood silently for some moments looking upon His redeemed saints, their countenances radiant with glory. He again welcomed the vast multitudes, and speaking of what was now theirs, and of joys to come later, said in His rich, musical voice, "I behold the travail of My soul, and am satisfied. This rich glory is yours to enjoy eternally. Your sorrows are ended. There shall be no more death, neither sorrow nor crying, neither shall there be any more pain." He continued by saying that we had kept the commandments of God and had a right to the tree of life.[47] We recalled His words of many years ago, which we were sure that He was applying to each one of us, "Well done, good and faithful servant; thou hast been faithful over a few things, I will make thee ruler over many things; enter thou into the joy of thy lord."[48]

Then followed the climax of this welcoming ceremony. Christ, the second Adam, looked with love toward the first Adam, standing head and shoulders over most of us, and beckoned him. We knew

HOME AT LAST!

what was coming, and there rang out upon the air an exultant cry of adoration. The two Adams were about to meet. As the father of our race moved forward, the Son of God stood with outstretched arms to receive him, the being whom He had created, who had sinned against his Maker, and for whose sin the marks of the crucifixion were plainly visible upon the Saviour's form. As Adam discerned the prints of the cruel nails, he did not fall upon the bosom of his Lord, but in humiliation cast himself at His feet. Tenderly the Saviour lifted him up, spoke comforting words of cheer, and bade him look once more upon the Eden home from which he had been exiled so long before.[49]

As this took place, we bowed and cast our own crowns at the feet of Jesus, who bade us stand. Then we touched our golden harps, and once more heaven was filled with rich music honoring the Lamb.

Jesus then guided us to the tree of life, which was nearby, and again we heard Him say in a lovely voice, richer than any music that ever fell on mortal ear, "The leaves of this tree are for the healing of the nations. Eat ye all of it."[50]

How happy we were! Oh, the wonders of redeeming love, the rapture of that hour when we met Jesus and His Father, realizing that once more, after so many millenniums, the human was in harmony with the divine.[51] With hearts made pure, with lips undefiled, we sang the riches of redeeming love. We entered the promised rest granted by God, with Jesus ready to lead us to the green pastures, by the streams of living waters that made glad the City of God.[52]

Our journey was ended. We were home at last!

References

[1] *Selected Messages*, book 2, p. 260.

[2] *In Heavenly Places*, p. 353; *The Desire of Ages*, p. 804; *The Great Controversy*, p. 645; *The SDA Bible Commentary*, Ellen G. White Comments, on 1 Cor. 15:42-52, p. 1093.

[3] *The SDA Bible Commentary*, Ellen G. White Comments, on 1 Cor 15:42-52, p. 1093; Letter 79, 1898; manuscript 36, 1906; *The Desire of Ages*, p. 804.

[4] *Our High Calling*, p. 367.

[5] *In Heavenly Places*, p. 367; *Thoughts From the Mount of Blessing*, p. 27.

[6] *The SDA Bible Commentary*, Ellen G. White Comments, on I Cor. 15:51-55, p. 1093.

[7] Isa. 53:11, *ibid*.

[8] *The Great Controversy*, p. 652.

[9] 2 Thess. 2:8.

[10] Rom. 7:12; *Sons and Daughters of God*, p. 361.

[11] *Early Writings*, p. 41.

[12] *Life Sketches*, p. 66; *Early Writings*, p. 17.

[13] *Early Writings*, p. 110. Revelation 8:1 refers to a period of one-half hour of silence in heaven as the seventh seal was opened. This, phrased in prophetic language, is seven and a half days in actual time. Since it took seven days for the trip from earth to heaven, one-half day remained for the journey from heaven to earth.

[14] *Early Writings*, pp. 287, 288; *Life Sketches*, p. 103.

[15] *The Great Controversy*, pp. 644, 645.

[16] *Education*, pp. 304, 305.
[17] *Maranatha*, p. 309.
[18] *The SDA Bible Commentary*, Ellen G. White Comments, on Gen. 3:15; p. 1084.
[19] *Ibid.*, Ellen G. White Comments, on Rev. 20:9, 10, 14, p. 986.
[20] Gen. 5:1-22; *ibid.*, vol. 1, p. 248.
[21] Heb. 11:5; *Testimonies*, vol. 8, p. 331.
[22] *Early Writings*, p. 40.
[23] Jude 9; *The Desire of Ages*, p. 421.
[24] *The Desire of Ages*, p. 421; *The SDA Bible Commentary*, on 2 Kings 2:1, p. 849; vol. 2, p. 77.
[25] *Prophets and Kings*, pp. 263, 264.
[26] *Early Writings*, pp. 16, 40.
[27] *Life Sketches*, p. 242.
[28] *Selected Messages*, book 2, pp. 259, 260.
[29] *Spiritual Gifts*, vol. 2, pp. 111, 112; *Life Sketches*, pp. 121-123.
[30] *Life Sketches*, p. 67; *Early Writings*, p. 17.
[31] Letter of Mrs. E. G. White to J. N. Andrews, 1878, quoted in Virgil Robinson, *John Nevins Andrews, Flame for the Lord* (Washington, D.C.: Review and Herald, 1975), pp. 37, 38, 76, 111, 112.
[32] *The Great Controversy*, p. 546; *Education*, p. 157; *The Adventist Home*, p. 536.
[33] Luke 23:42, 43; *The Desire of Ages*, pp. 749, 750; *Early Writings*, p. 258.
[34] Heb. 11:8, 16; Luke 13:28; Job 19:26; *Selected Messages*, book 1, p. 64; *The Great Controversy*, p. 667.
[35] Luke 13:28.
[36] *Christ's Object Lessons*, pp. 71, 72.
[37] Matt. 25:40; *The Desire of Ages*, p. 638.
[38] *My Life Today*, p. 353; *Fundamentals of Christian Education*, p. 90.
[39] *The Great Controversy*, p. 647.
[40] *Testimonies*, vol. 2, pp. 697, 698.
[41] *Early Writings*, p. 288.
[42] *The Great Controversy*, pp. 650, 665.
[43] Rev. 14:1-5; 15:3; *ibid.*, p. 649.
[44] Chap. 2:17; *ibid.*, pp. 646, 650; *Child Guidance*, pp. 569, 564; *Selected Messages*, book 2, p. 260; *Early Writings*, p. 288.
[45] *Maranatha*, p. 342; *Life Sketches*, p. 66; *Early Writings*, p. 16.
[46] *Early Writings*, pp. 17, 288.
[47] Rev. 14:12; 22:14; *ibid.*, pp. 17, 288, 289; *Life Sketches*, pp. 67, 103.
[48] Matt. 25:23.
[49] *The Great Controversy*, p. 647.
[50] *Early Writings*, p. 289.
[51] *The Great Controversy*, p. 646.
[52] *"That I May Know Him,"* p. 371.

Chapter Four

The Capital City

After the welcoming ceremony in the center of the Holy City, guardian angels took their charges to the mansions that Jesus had prepared for them, where they were to live during the next thousand years.[1] As the book of life had been checked during the investigative judgment, each one of the redeemed had been assigned a place in heaven. The homes to which we were taken by our angel companions were most beautiful, reflecting the glory of God emanating from the central part of the city.[2]

In spite of the long journey just completed, we were not tired. How wonderful it was to realize that we never again would be fatigued. There was no desire to sleep, and in the city itself no night ever came to encourage slumber.[3]

We found our homes large and commodious. We had, of course, been used to ceilings between eight and ten feet high, but our mansions were between twenty and twenty-five feet in height, constructed so that they would be suitable when we eventually grew to the ideal stature of mankind as we had seen in Adam earlier that day.[4] There were beautiful flowers and a fine lawn around each place. As we looked down the street we noticed that Jesus had thoughtfully provided homes for the loved ones who had come with us. We waved to them and to some of our friends as their angels guided them to their homes farther down the avenue.

Our angel friends left my companion and me to enjoy our mansions for a while, knowing that we would want to spend some time by ourselves. We walked through the various rooms exclaiming over the fine facilities. We were overjoyed and thankful for what we saw. We would have been satisfied with much less! Then we walked out to the avenue and down the way to see how our loved ones had

THE CAPITAL CITY

fared. Together, we commented excitedly among ourselves about the wonderful things that had been prepared for us. Our special angel companions returned shortly after we arrived back at our home. They showed us some features about the house that we had not noticed, things that we had never seen on earth. Then we sat together in front and ate of the fruit that grew on some nearby trees.

After a while one of us asked, "Would it be possible to visit some part of the city?"

One of the guardian angels answered, "Why, surely! We'll show you around!"

"Could we invite our parents and some friends to go along?"

"Yes. We all can go together."

So we went to the homes of our dear ones and told them what we were planning to do. They accepted the invitation right away. When others who lived near saw us preparing to go out, they joined us, and with a corresponding number of angels leading us, the large group moved down the avenue in the general direction of the center of the city. Beautiful homes, with ample space between them, lined the thoroughfares on both sides. The pavement of the streets was of pure, transparent gold that looked like glass and reflected the brilliance that pervaded the entire city.[5]

To describe what we saw as we traveled toward the center of the Holy City is impossible. Words had failed others who in times past had seen these glories. Isaiah and Paul, for example, had said, "Eye hath not seen, nor ear heard, neither have entered into the heart of man, the things which God hath prepared for them that love him."[6] Ellen White had written, "My powers would be inadequate to do this [describe the things concerning the New Jerusalem] or even make an approach. . . . The most eloquent representation of the New Jerusalem . . . [is but a feeble attempt to present it]. Your power as an artist will, when stretched to its utmost capacity, fall down faint and weary in seeking to take in the things of the unseen world, and yet there is an eternity beyond. . . . Let the imaginations of the people be on the highest stretch to contemplate the glories of the New Jerusalem and yet they have but just entered upon the borders of the eternal weight of glory that shall be realized by the faithful overcomer."[7]

Mrs. White repeated this observation in other statements:

HOME AT LAST!

"Human language is inadequate to describe the reward of the righteous. It will be known only to those who behold it. No finite mind can comprehend the glory of the Paradise of God."[8] "Language is altogether too feeble to attempt a description of heaven. As the scene rises before me, I am lost in amazement. Carried away with the surpassing splendor and excellent glory, I lay down the pen, and exclaim, 'Oh, what love! what wondrous love!' The most exalted language fails to describe the glory of heaven or the matchless depths of a Saviour's love."[9] And again, "You cannot paint, you cannot picture, and the martyr tongue cannot begin to give any description of the glory of the future life."[10]

A faint idea, only a partial revelation, of what our Father had prepared for us had been gleaned through His Word.[11] All that was beautiful on the sin-tainted earth had been a reminder to us of what we might expect.[12] We now realized that the time on earth had been our winter, with the chilly winds of affliction blowing upon us and the waves of trouble rolling against us. But now we were enjoying eternal summer. All trials were over. There would be no more of the sad happenings that had tried us before. We now understood that the earth had been a place of preparation for what now we were enjoying, and that God's promise had been completely fulfilled.[13]

The city was very large. We were informed that it was laid out in a perfect square, and that each side was almost 350 terrestrial miles [560 kilometers] long. Our own houses were located far from the center, where was situated the government of the universe, but distances now were not a factor as they had been on earth. Motion was not limited to walking speed, for we glided along, covering space more rapidly. Nevertheless we tended to move slowly so that we could appreciate the beauties that we had only glimpsed when we had entered the capital earlier. Now we stopped from time to time to admire one scene and then another. We were mostly silent, for we found no words in our heretofore limited vocabulary to describe the panorama.

Moving along, we eventually came to a tree-lined river, which had the appearance of a sea of glass. It flowed down the center of the boulevard in this section of the city. Our angels told us that this was a part of the river of life, and that it had its source in a spring under the large hill in the center of the city where God's throne and abode were located. We could see our reflections in the crystal-clear water. The angels added that the waters of that spring flowed out in four directions, dividing the city into four sections.[14] Each of the four streams ran down the center of a wide avenue.

On each side of the river stood the tree of life, which had been transferred with the Garden of Eden just before the Flood. Beyond it were many other beautiful trees that also bore fruit. But the tree of life surpassed in glory all other trees.[15] We already knew that this tree produced fruit every month, and that we would partake of it freely. This fruit had the appearance of apples of gold and silver. Actually, there were many kinds of fruits, including manna, figs, pomegranates, and grapes.[16] The leaves of the tree were sweeter than honey and were an antidote of death, sustaining life and immortality. They possessed healing powers and had the ability to drive away all faintheartedness.[17] The fruit had the power of giving immortal vigor, of perpetuating life. It was for this reason that when sin entered Eden, God had no longer allowed men to partake of the fruit. Even then, the fact that Adam and Eve had eaten of it protracted their lives and the lives of their antediluvian offspring to almost a millennium. But gradually, as vitality decreased, the life span was shortened to six hundred, four hundred, one-hundred-twenty, and finally to seventy years. Had the Lord not returned, life eventually would have become extinct.[18]

Remembering another tree that had been placed in the first Garden of Eden, we asked our angel friends about the tree of knowledge of good and evil. They answered that there was no such tree in heaven to provide opportunity for temptation. No tempter was present and there was no possibility of wrongdoing.[19] They added that the tree had been placed in other worlds, but the inhabitants of those worlds had been obedient to the Father's commands.[20]

As we approached the center, we came to what appeared to be a park. Actually, it was the Garden of Eden. We took a long time going through the garden, appreciating the fact that our ancestors, Adam and Eve, with their own hands had trained the plants before being cast out.[21] At the time of our visit, many others also were going through the Garden. In fact, the entire city through which we had passed was teeming with activity.

My angel pointed out a fine-looking man standing under some

HOME AT LAST!

vines at one part of the park and identified him as Daniel.[22] He was talking with a distinguished-looking gentleman who looked to us as we had imagined Nebuchadnezzar of Babylon, that formerly proud king who at the close of his life had finally been thoroughly converted. One of the accompanying angels confirmed our supposition.[23] Farther down the way we saw the apostle Paul in conversation with Peter.[24]

We finally arrived in the center of the city and moved up the high but gently sloping hill. From there we were able to look over the entire city with eyes that were much stronger than those we had possessed when we had been on earth. It was a huge metropolis, covering close to 120,000 square miles. As we looked, it was hard to realize that the city covered an area about the size of what had been the State of New Mexico in the United States of America. The redeemed who came from Europe could easily compare it in area to the countries they had known as Norway or Poland.

We had sometimes wondered where everyone would be located in the Holy City, but now realized that if each individual had a fairly large plot of land, about fifteen thousand square feet, there would be room for more than 200 million homes in the city itself, not including what could be provided outside the city.

As far as eye could see there was an intermingling of beautiful homes, green trees, the brilliant colors of flowers and bushes, wide avenues, and a combination of other things that pleased every sense. Beyond the walls we could see the suburbs.[25]

By this time a good long while had passed, so we all returned to our homes, leaving other sectors of the city as well as the outskirts to be visited later. We knew that there would be no lack of time.

After a few days had passed, we gathered a group of our loved ones and some of our closest friends for another walk with our angel friends. On the way we visited, exchanging impressions and listening to new information and further explanations from our celestial companions. This time they guided us away from the center of the city. We walked down a broad avenue and through one of the gates on the south wall of the city in order to obtain a panoramic view of the capital from the outside. There we saw what we had read about in the apostle John's description of the Holy City in the book of Revelation. As we stood on a little hill, we gazed at the great walls, complementing well the 350-mile extent of each side.[26]

THE CAPITAL CITY

We observed that the walls were built on twelve foundations, and that God's light from the center of the city that shone through these made them resemble a huge rainbow, except that the colors lay in horizontal lines. From previous knowledge combined with the additional explanations of the angels, and what we could see with our own eyes, we knew that each one of the foundations was made of precious stones. Each foundation, each layer of precious stones, bore the name of one of Jesus' twelve disciples: Simon Peter, Andrew, James, John, Philip, Bartholomew, Thomas, Matthew, James (the son of Alphaeus), Thaddaeus, Simon (the Canaanite), and Matthias.[27] The stones that made up these twelve foundations, in order, were: jasper, sky-blue sapphire, greenish chalcedony, bright-green emerald, sardonyx (red and brown against a white background), reddish sardius, yellowish chrysolite, sea-green beryl, yellowish topaz, apple-green chrysoprasus, lavender hued jacinth, and royal purple amethyst.[28]

As we moved farther into the outlying areas for a better panoramic view, we noticed that there were three gates in the wall facing us. Our angels told us that each one of the four walls of the city had three gates, a total of twelve. Each gate was a single, huge pearl, which hung on glittering hinges.[29] Over each gate was the name of one of the tribes of Israel. With our keen sight we could read the names over the gates in the south wall facing us: the gate of Simeon, the gate of Issachar, and the gate of Zebulun. Since we could only see these three, our angel friends completed our information by giving us the names over the gates on the other three walls: opposite us, on the north side, were the gates of Judah, Reuben, and Levi; on the east side to our right were the gates of Joseph, Benjamin, and Manasseh; and on the west side, to our left, were the gates of Gad, Asher, and Naphtali.[30]

There was an angel watchman at each gate, although this was really an honorary position.[31] In previous times, when angels were commissioned to run errands to the earth, they had presented golden cards to the watchmen as they left, but this was not necessary now.[32] Since it was always day, the gates were never closed. The walls themselves were there for beauty, with no other special purpose since there was nothing around that had to be kept out. They were a convenient place where residents of the city could go for a panoramic view of what was going on outside, or a general view of the beautiful

HOME AT LAST!

city inside.[33]

On earth we had been accustomed to having churches somewhere near us. We had read of the sanctuary and its services, and of the Temple in old Jerusalem. Now, however, we observed that the heavenly temple was not located within the Holy City, the reason being that God Himself was in the city and that we could have direct and open communion with the Father, the Son, and the Holy Ghost.[34] The temple, which had been the pattern for the earthly sanctuary and temples, was located outside the city on beautiful Mount Zion, which itself was surrounded by seven flower-covered mountains. There were some woods not far away.[35]

The temple was supported by seven pillars, all of transparent gold, set with most glorious pearls. We moved toward the shining edifice. Those of us who were members of the special group of 144,000 were shown the interior of the temple by Jesus Himself, while the others walked around the outside area as they waited. We passed through a door and found a veil blocking the view. When it was raised, we entered the holy place. There, in the midst of a halo of glory, we saw the altar of incense, the candlestick with seven lamps, and the table of shewbread. The holy place was separated from the Most Holy Place by another veil. Jesus raised this second veil, and we stepped into the Holy of Holies.

In it we saw an ark. Its top and sides were of purest gold, and on each end was a cherub with its wings spread out over the ark. The cherub's faces were turned toward each other, and they looked downward. Between them was a golden censer. Prior to His second return to the earth, Jesus had stood by the ark, and as our prayers had ascended to Him, the incense in the censer would smoke, and He would offer up our prayers with the smoke of the incense to His Father.

In the ark we saw the golden pot of manna, Aaron's rod that budded, and the original tables of stone, which folded together like a book. Jesus opened them, and we saw the Ten Commandments, which had been written with the finger of God. We noticed that the first four were brighter than the last six, and that the fourth was the brightest of all. There were also tables of stone on which the names of the 144,000 were engraved in letters of gold.[36]

As we left the temple and looked toward the city, we could see

THE CAPITAL CITY

beyond the walls the beautiful tree-lined avenues, all leading to the central high area. How happy we were to know that the throne of God, the very center of the universe, was with us forever. We could see above that sacred place a most beautiful rainbow, the everlasting testimony of God's great love to man.[37]

References

[1] John 14:1-3.
[2] Manuscript 31, 1901.
[3] Rev. 22:5; 21:25.
[4] *Spiritual Gifts*, vol. 3, p. 84.
[5] Verse 21; *Counsels to Parents and Teachers*, p. 63.
[6] Isa. 64:4; 1 Cor. 2:9.
[7] Letter 54, April 4, 1886, quoted in *Adventist Review*, June 18, 1981.
[8] *The Great Controversy*, p. 675.
[9] *Early Writings*, p. 289.
[10] *The SDA Bible Commentary*, Ellen G. White Comments, on 2 Tim. 3:16, p. 920.
[11] *Education*, p. 301.
[12] *Counsels to Parents and Teachers*, p. 55; *Testimonies*, vol. 7, p. 76.
[13] *The SDA Bible Commentary*, Ellen G. White Comments, on Rev. 21:4, p. 988.
[14] Gen. 2:10; Eze. 47:1, 2; *Testimonies*, vol. 8, p. 254.
[15] Rev. 22:1, 2; *Life Sketches*, p. 67; *Early Writings*, p. 289; *Patriarchs and Prophets*, p. 47; *My Life Today*, p. 355.
[16] *Spiritual Gifts*, vol. 2, p. 55; *Patriarchs and Prophets*, p. 47; *Early Writings*, p. 289; *The Adventist Home*, p. 542; *The Great Controversy*, p. 675.
[17] *The SDA Bible Commentary*, Ellen G. White Comments, on Rev. 22:2, p. 989; *My Life Today*, p. 355; *The Desire of Ages*, p. 366.
[18] *Patriarchs and Prophets*, pp. 60, 62; *The Great Controversy*, p. 533; *The SDA Bible Commentary*, Ellen G. White Comments, on Rev. 22:2, p. 988.
[19] Nahum 1:9; *Education*, p. 302.
[20] *Early Writings*, p. 40; *The Adventist Home*, p. 543.
[21] *The Great Controversy*, pp. 646-648.
[22] *Selected Messages*, book 1, p. 64.
[23] *The SDA Bible Commentary*, Ellen G. White Comments, on Dan. 4:37, p. 1170; *Prophets and Kings*, p. 521.
[24] *The Great Controversy*, p. 667.
[25] Eze. 48:17.
[26] Rev. 21:16, 17.
[27] Matt. 10:2-4; Acts 1:26; Rev. 21:14.
[28] Rev. 21:18-20.
[29] Verses 12, 13, 21.
[30] Chap. 7:5-8, Gen. 49:3-27; Eze. 48:31-34; Num. 2:3-31. The order in the four lists varies. For convenience we have used the order given by Ezekiel, substituting Mannaseh, Joseph's son, for Dan, in accordance with the list in Revelation. Joseph's portion was thus double the others. Dan was excluded possibly because of its idolatrous reputation (Judges 18:30, 31) and its treachery (Gen. 49:17).
[31] Rev. 21:12.
[32] Verse 25; *Early Writings*, p. 39.
[33] Verse 25.
[34] Verse 22; *The Great Controversy*, p. 676.
[35] *Spiritual Gifts*, vol. 2, pp. 54, 55; *Early Writings*, pp. 18, 19.
[36] *The Great Controversy*, pp. 434, 435; *Early Writings*, pp. 19, 32, 33; *Spiritual Gifts*, vol. 2, pp. 54, 55.
[37] *Maranatha*, p. 326.

Chapter Five

The First Thousand Years

Not long after our arrival in the Holy City, we saw and took part in the fulfillment of one of Jesus' great desires, expressed to His disciples the night before His death: "I will not drink henceforth of this fruit of the vine, until that day when I drink it new with you in my Father's kingdom."[1]

The time had come. We, the redeemed, were in the mansions that He had prepared for us. Now came the long-awaited repast. Jesus sat at a table of pure silver, many miles in length. Adam and Eve, the prophets of old, the disciples, and all the other redeemed were seated with Him. In spite of its length, our eyes could see the entire table. We saw the fruit of the tree of life on it, and after the blessing, we all partook of that which Jesus gave us.[2]

Touring the city and its suburbs, visiting our loved ones and friends, and working in and about our mansions, we found a good part of our time well occupied. Nevertheless, during this thousand-year period the Lord had a task for us to do, and this took up a portion of each day. It was not the happiest of tasks, but it had to be done.

Our own personal sorrows and sadness, brought on by the weaknesses of our earthly natures, had been wiped away at the time of the resurrection and the translation, and grief caused by personal losses was no more. But during this period of one thousand years and even for a while afterward there still was sorrow—the tears and heartaches that the Father, the Son, and the angels had undergone during the millenniums since sin had entered the universe, sorrow over souls who had rejected divine aid and had chosen to be lost.[3] While happiness was now predominant, there still remained this trace of sadness. Tears brought on by this kind of sorrow would be wiped away only after the total eradication of sin.[4]

We had been surprised to find that some of the good people we had known on earth were not with us in heaven,[5] and we wondered why. Our Saviour wanted us to know the reason. He desired us to come to a more complete understanding of His love and His justice, to know that it was being applied to all in an equal fashion. So during this period we were kept busy in the almost-final phase of God's judgment.

During the period of the existence of the earth accurate records had been kept of the lives of all who had lived. Every act, every secret thing, whether good or evil, had been recorded by attending angels.[6] These records were kept in what could be termed a daybook, the book of remembrance.[7] Depending on the decision made by each individual during his life, his name could be transferred to either of two other books, the book of life or the book of death.

The book of remembrance covered the total record of each individual from birth until death. It was, as it were, a faithful picture of his character as accurately portrayed as when an artist paints the likeness of the human features. Everything good was recorded by the angels—words spoken, deeds done, faithful acts of love performed, every act of righteousness attempted, every temptation resisted, every evil overcome, every word of tender pity expressed, every sacrifice made, every suffering and sorrow endured for Christ's sake, every heartache caused by sin or oppression, every longing for a higher spiritual life, and every desire for a closer walk with God. Motives for actions were also taken into consideration.[8] Even the gestures and facial expressions were mirrored there.[9] Tears for sins committed were set down, and our wanderings were recorded.[10]

On the other hand, the book of remembrance also contained the complete angelic record of the rebellion, the sins, and all hidden selfishness of individuals. Registered there were every wrong word, every selfish action, every unfulfilled duty, every secret sin, every artful dissembling, heaven's warnings or reproofs neglected, moments wasted, opportunities unimproved, and the wrong use of influence.[11] The acts of every day, recorded in this book, depicted the character of the person, and pointed out decisions made by him that determined future eternal life or future eternal death. Since God reads the heart and does not judge solely by the exterior,[12] He also had taken into consideration such factors as where a person was born, his heredity, and his environment.[13]

The book of life was the book of honor, the highest award that could be conferred upon a human being. In it were listed the names of those who had been redeemed.[14] In this book were placed the names of all who had ever professed the name of Christ, all who had served the Lord, who had been His faithful servants, and who had reached ever heavenward for help.[15] Their good-deeds part of this record was, of course, also found in the daybook, the book of remembrance. The book of life had been the basis of careful investigation during the period that began in 1844 and ended with the close of probation.

Beginning with the righteous dead and continuing on through the living, we looked carefully at each name to ascertain whether or not that person had accepted the righteousness of Christ, and then given evidence of this acceptance by a changed life. If the verdict had been favorable, his name had remained in this book. His sins, no matter how many or how onerous, had been blotted out by the blood of Jesus. God, the Judge, had seen Christ's perfect life in him, and he had been included in the group of the redeemed.

If, on the other hand, the person had grown weary of well-doing and what he thought were excessive sacrifices, and had forsaken Christ, his name had been blotted out of the book of life. Now his record in the book of remembrance revealed only sins committed, including details of pride, selfishness, and all the works of the flesh.[16] If there had been no hearkening to the call of the Holy Spirit before the close of probation, his name was then transferred to the book of death, to be added to the list of those who had never called on Christ.

Those of us who now participated in this next-to-last phase of judgment would not be using the book of life, though we could look into it as a matter of interest. It had been used from 1844 onward, and was closed when Jesus left the Most Holy Place and declared that probation time had ended. When this happened, the case of every individual from Adam to the last child born before Christ's second coming had been decided, either for eternal life or eternal death.[17]

Our task during the thousand years in heaven demanded concentration on the third book, the book of death. It contained the long list of those who had never called upon Christ, who had never believed in Him, and who had resisted and fought Him during their lives. It also included those who had once accepted Christ but had finally forsaken Him. Their actions, their lives, and their sins were all recorded there. They could have had eternal life, but they had chosen death.[18] They themselves had made this decision. After the close of probation, there was no more opportunity to change.[19]

The first name on the list was Satan, the originator of sin. This was followed by the names of his angel followers, and then by all the innumerable hosts of those who had chosen Satan as their leader. Jesus had indicated that He wanted us to participate with Him in this work of judgment, that of deciding each case according to the deeds done in the body, and meting out to those listed in the book of death the portion that they must suffer according to their works as written in this book, as compared with the statute book, the Word of God. It was not necessary for everyone to go through the record of every single individual from the beginning of the earth onward, but each one of us particularly sought out the names of those in whom we had specific interest, and then helped in the decisions affecting other individuals.

Many of us had wondered why certain highly respected members of our church were not with us in heaven. Why wasn't a well-known leader here? Why wasn't one of our cousins, a loved aunt, even a husband, a parent, or a certain child in heaven? They had professed to serve the Lord. Why weren't they here with us?

As we went through the books, there were many astonishing disclosures. Men and women did not appear as they had looked to our human eyes and finite judgment. Secret sins were now laid open to the view of any and all. Motives and intentions that had been hidden in the dark chambers of the heart were revealed. All appeared as a real-life picture. As we compared notes with our companions, we talked of surprises found in our investigations: the unfaithfulness of husbands to their wives, or in other cases the disloyalty of wives to their husbands. Parents, wondering why some of their children had not been saved, learned for the first time what was the real character of those children. On the other hand, some young people who missed their parents now saw the errors and mistakes that had marked the lives of their fathers and mothers. Men who, though posing as followers of Christ, had robbed their neighbors through false representations, were now exposed. They had not escaped with their ill-gotten gains. In the book of death we found an exact record of

HOME AT LAST!

every unjust account and every unfair dealing.[20]

On the other hand, we had been somewhat surprised to see persons in heaven whom we had not expected to see. There were some who had known little of theology, but who had cherished God's principles. Through the influence of the Holy Spirit they had been a blessing to all around them. There were those whom we had called heathen, but who had cherished the spirit of kindness. Before hearing the gospel, they had befriended missionaries, even ministering to them at the peril of their own lives. Among them were some who had worshiped God ignorantly, those to whom the light had never been brought by human instrumentality. Though ignorant of the written law of God, they had heard His voice speaking to them in nature, and had done what the law required. Their works were evidence that the Holy Spirit had touched their hearts, and they were recognized as the children of the heavenly Father.[21]

As we drew conclusions from the study of many cases, we realized that God's decisions were right and just. Even as we had come out of the graves or been translated with the same thoughts and attitudes as we had had on earth, so it was with those whose names were in the book of death. There was no change of character when Christ came. Character building had continued while probation lasted, but had then ceased. As these people went into their graves, so they would emerge later. Their enmity to Christ and their rebellious spirit would not change. What they had enjoyed before they would miss if they could not have it in the future.[22]

Could they enter heaven, to dwell forever with those whom they had despised and hated on earth? Truth would never be agreeable to a liar. Meekness would be abhorrent to the proud. Disinterested love would not appear attractive to the selfish. What source of enjoyment could heaven offer to those who had been wholly absorbed in earthly and selfish interests? What pleasure would they derive out of worship, when they had disliked religious activities on earth?

Should those whose lives had been spent in rebellion against God be transported to heaven and witness the high, the holy state of perfection that ever exists there, with everybody happy and praising the Lord? Should those whose hearts had been filled with hatred of God and His truth and holiness mingle with the heavenly throng? They would neither want nor be able to join in the songs of praise.

THE FIRST THOUSAND YEARS

They could not endure the glory of God the Father and of His Son. Their lives of rebellion against God had unfitted them for heaven, and they would want to flee from that holy place, for they would not feel comfortable there. They would welcome destruction. We came to understand that their exclusion from heaven was voluntary, their own willful choice, and was just and merciful on the part of God.[23]

After studying the records and comparing the lives of those recorded in the book of death with the Word of God, together with Christ we determined the amount of punishment to be meted out to each individual when final judgment was executed. This punishment was then written opposite the name of that person. All were concerned with the punishment of Satan and his angels. The sentence pronounced on Satan himself was far greater than that of his angels and those whom he had deceived. After all these had perished, he was to live and suffer on much longer.[24]

While we kept ourselves occupied and happy during this period of a thousand years, the situation on the earth that we had left was one of complete misery. The appearance of the planet itself was almost indescribable. At the time of the second coming of Christ, the mountains had burned like a furnace and poured forth terrible streams of lava, destroying gardens and fields, villages and cities. As they poured their melted ore, rocks, and heated mud into the rivers, these had boiled like a pot and sent forth massive rocks, scattering their broken fragments upon the land with incomparable violence. Entire rivers had dried up. The earth had been convulsed, and there had been dreadful eruptions and earthquakes everywhere. God had sent terrible plagues that had destroyed many of the wicked.[25]

Now the earth looked like a desolate wilderness. Cities and villages, shaken by the earthquakes, lay in heaps. Mountains had been moved from their foundations leaving large caverns. Ragged rocks, thrown out by the sea or torn out of the earth itself, were scattered over its surface. Large trees had been uprooted and were strewn over the land. The picture described by Jeremiah so many centuries before had now been completely fulfilled.[26]

There was no human being left upon the earth. After the redeemed were delivered and taken up into heaven, those who were still alive on earth, those who had chosen Satan as their leader, those who had listened to and accepted the teachings of their false leaders,

HOME AT LAST!

turned their anger upon one another. The earth seemed deluged with blood, and dead bodies were scattered from one end of it to the other. The remnant of the wicked who had not been destroyed by the plagues and the violence, had been consumed with the spirit of the Lord's mouth and destroyed by the brightness of His glory.[27]

This, then, was the situation that Satan and his angels faced after almost six thousand years of their reign. This was now their home during the thousand-year period while we were rejoicing in the capital city in heaven. Satan was not permitted to leave the boundaries of the earth, being in this sense chained, or bound to it—somewhat like a house arrest. He did not have the privilege of going to other planets, to tempt and annoy those who had never fallen. The sins of God's people that he had caused had now been placed upon him, and he was pronounced guilty of them. As in the days of the sanctuary services in Israel the scapegoat had been sent away into a land not inhabited, so Satan was banished to the desolate earth, to that uninhabited and dreary wilderness.

During this time, while the devil wandered to and fro beholding the results of his rebellion against the law of God, his sufferings were intense. Since he had been cast out of heaven, his life of unceasing activity had banished all reflection. But now, deprived of his power, he was left to contemplate the part that he had acted. He looked with trembling and terror to the dreadful future, when he must suffer for all the evil that he had done.[28]

But he knew and we knew that he would still have one more opportunity to destroy Christ and the righteous. There would be one more final demonstration of what he really was. He would still be loosed for a season.[29]

References

[1] Matt. 26:29.
[2] *Early Writings*, p. 19.
[3] *The Desire of Ages*, pp. 356, 588; *Selected Messages*, book 1, p. 76; *Testimonies*, vol. 9, p. 286.
[4] Rev. 21:1-4.
[5] *Christ's Object Lessons*, pp. 71, 72.
[6] Dan. 7:10; 1 Cor. 6:2; Eccl. 12:14.
[7] Mal. 3:16.
[8] *The Great Controversy*, pp. 481, 486.
[9] Isa. 3:9.
[10] Ps. 56:8.
[11] Isa. 65:2, 6, 7; *The Great Controversy*, p. 482.
[12] I Sam. 16:7; Ps. 44:21.
[13] Ps. 87:4-6.

[14] Luke 10:19, 20.
[15] Phil. 4:3; *The Great Controversy*, p. 480.
[16] Ps. 69:28; Rev. 13:8; 17:8.
[17] *The Great Controversy*, p. 490.
[18] Jer. 17:13; 2:22; Job 14:17; Deut. 32:32-36; Hosea 13:12.
[19] *The Great Controversy*, p. 490.
[20] *Maranatha*, p. 340; *Early Writings*, pp. 290, 291.
[21] *The Desire of Ages*, p. 638.
[22] *The Great Controversy*, p. 662; *The SDA Bible Commentary*, Ellen G. White Comments, on Rev. 22:14, p. 990.
[23] *The Great Controversy*, p. 543; *Steps to Christ*, pp. 17, 18.
[24] *Early Writings*, p. 291.
[25] *Ibid.*, pp. 285, 286; *The Great Controversy*, pp. 636-644.
[26] Jer. 4:23-27; *Early Writings*, p. 290.
[27] Verse 25; *The Great Controversy*, p. 657; *Early Writings*, pp. 289, 290.
[28] Rev. 20:1-3; *Early Writings*, p. 290; *The Great Controversy*, pp. 658, 661.
[29] Verse 3.

Chapter Six

Changing Concepts

During the thousand years that we resided in the heavenly capital, our thinking, our concepts, went through a process of transition. Since our thought processes at the time of translation had continued unbroken in our new environment,[1] we had had to adjust to situations that were now changed. This was particularly the case with that which had to do with time, distance, space, and size.

During the first fifteen hundred years of man's existence on the earth he had measured everything in relation to the fact that his life was limited to a time just short of one thousand years. Then, after the Flood, the amount of time granted him was reduced to a few hundred years, and by the time that Jacob's sons were living in Egypt, this period had been reduced to just a bit more than one century. Life expectancy was shortened still further in succeeding generations. In the fifteenth century B.C. Moses wrote, "The days of our years are threescore years and ten; and if by reason of strength they be fourscore years, yet is their strength labour and sorrow."[2] This situation had continued during the millenniums until Jesus returned to take us home, and was the period by which we had measured all our activities. Anything that we attempted, any trips that we wished to make, any tasks that we wished to accomplish, had to be tailored within the time span of our seventy to eighty years on earth. This had even affected the thinking of many concerning promises that our Lord had made concerning His "immediate" return.

Even the matter of distance had been affected by the limitations of time. During the first centuries of earth's history, whether a place was near or far was determined by how long it took to reach it by walking or running. This might differ according to the height of a man or woman, for it determined how long or short his steps would be. His

52

CHANGING CONCEPTS

weight and his strength could also vary his speed, and thus might increase or decrease the time needed to make the journey.

Then a new element came in that "shortened" distances by reducing traveling time. Man tamed horses, mules, camels, oxen, llamas, and other animals, and subjected these to his will. He used them for personal travel and for carrying loads. A horse, for example, could move more than twice as fast as a man, thus cutting down on time needed to cover a given distance. Now man's horizon expanded to cover a larger distance. How far could he ride a horse and come back home? This improvement of transportational facilities became standard for several thousands of years, continuing until the last centuries of earth's existence.

Then the harnessing of steam and other natural elements came into play. Man developed the train, which now picked up at the speed of a galloping horse, and gradually reduced the concept of far and near by speeding along at scores of miles per hour.

After that, the airplane was converted into a common carrier for man and his goods. The plane picked up from the speeding train, and as jet power came into use, this velocity was multiplied five or six times. When this was increased by the use of spacecraft, the speed, by human standards, was so great that its measurement was changed from miles per hour to Machs (the ratio of the speed of a body to the speed of sound in the surrounding medium through which the body is moving). The plane had made the entire world accessible to man, but spacecraft made it feasible for him to journey outside the world, even reaching the moon and approaching some planets through unmanned exploration.

In less than a century, the time needed to cross a three-thousand-mile continent was cut from several months to the fourth part of a day by jet plane, and to just a few minutes by spacecraft.

In our own day-to-day life on earth the concept of distance had also varied according to the time that it took to do a job. The task of trimming the grass was greatly reduced in time and effort by the use of a riding mower instead of one pushed by hand. The size of our garden and the length of the vegetable rows seemed great when taken care of by digging and hoeing, but the work became almost pleasant when we used a rototiller, or a tractor pulling a plow or a drill.

The same applied to size. Our own height and age affected our

HOME AT LAST!

judgment on this matter. What we saw as tall mountains when we were children became hills when we saw them again as adults. A person who looked like a giant when we were just little folks was reduced to normal size when our height reached his. And, as mentioned above, the earth itself appeared to be reduced in size with improved and speedier methods of transportation.

In heaven, these concepts were shifted once again as measurements of time and speed and even size were changed. We came to the realization and understanding that God's ways are not man's ways,[3] and that the Lord does not look at things as we do.[4] Where man had had to count his days,[5] God had no need of doing so, for a thousand years in His sight were as yesterday,[6] as one day; on the other hand, one day to Him might be the same as a thousand years.[7] In other words, time just is not a factor to the Lord.

This was a concept that we grasped, during the thousand years. Now we came to understand that the statement of many, "My Lord delayeth his coming,"[8] had no basis. When the Lord said "Quickly" concerning His return to the apostle Paul and to John the revelator, and even as our own pastor had understood and preached it, He meant exactly what He said. For Him it was "quickly," for a thousand years were as a day. To us, however, "quickly" meant something else, measured in terms of seventy to eighty years. The Lord actually had not delayed His coming. He had appointed a time.[9] God had always known the exact day and hour of His return. He knew this when Jesus was on earth.[10] For Him there had been no tarrying or delay.[11] We, in our ignorance, with our limited concepts, had misjudged Him, and because of this there had been those who began "to smite . . . [their] fellowservants, and to eat and drink with the drunken,"[12] losing their way.

Now, near the end of the thousand-year period in heaven, our concept of space, distance, and speed had adjusted to divine reality. After having covered trillions of miles in just seven days, we saw things in a different light. Now we did not have to measure time within the confines of fourscore years. A thousand years could seem like a day and a day as a thousand years. And so it was with this millennium in heaven. Time was not a factor in our lives. We always had something to do and were always busy.

It was during this period that we became aware of certain physical changes in ourselves. We were growing slowly from our earthly stature, which had been stunted because of the effects of sin, to our originally planned height.[13] At the same time we were also developing wings, which, of course, made it much easier to get from one place to another comfortably and in a hurry.[14]

This same process of growth was also visible in the infants that had been taken to their mothers' arms at the time of the resurrection, as well as in the children translated with their parents. Our concept of time and growth had now changed. On earth a little child had reached half his adult stature at the age of 2; now the process of growth, though steady, was much slower, even as it had been in the Garden of Eden and immediately afterward.[15] Furthermore, half-stature now was not around three feet, but was more like seven to eight feet, around half the stature of Adam, the first man.[16] It was thus that at the end of this period of one thousand years there were still children growing.[17]

In spite of all this, we should say that we had absolutely no trouble in adjusting our thinking, our concepts. We were filled with joy at being redeemed, were happy with all that we had found, and were perfectly satisfied with everything that the Lord had prepared for us. But there was much more awaiting us. The first thousand years were now almost over, and an entirely new page of history was being opened to us.

References

[1] *Education*, p. 307.
[2] Ps. 90:10.
[3] Isa. 55:8, 9.
[4] 1 Sam. 16:7.
[5] Ps. 90:12.
[6] Ps. 90:4.
[7] 2 Peter 3:8.
[8] Matt. 24:48.
[9] Dan. 8:19; 11:35.
[10] Matt. 24:36.
[11] Heb. 10:37.
[12] Matt. 24:49.
[13] *The Story of Redemption*, p. 21; *The Great Controversy*, p. 645.
[14] *Early Writings*, p. 53.
[15] Gen. 5:3-28. The average age of a father at the time of the birth of his first son before the Flood was 117, whereas in the last generations of earth's history it was around 24.
[16] *The Story of Redemption*, p. 21.
[17] *Spiritual Gifts*, vol. 2, p. 54.

Chapter Seven

The Last Battle

Toward the end of our thousand years in heaven we noticed an air of expectancy among the angels, which soon spread throughout the redeemed host. We already had a good idea of what was going to happen. During our lives on earth we had read about and had seen the moving of some capital cities such as those of Australia and Brazil. But this would be of a magnitude far surpassing anything we had known. New Jerusalem, the capital of the universe, would be transferred from its present location in the heavens to its new site on Planet Earth, the area that had been the focus of attention of the universe and its inhabitants during the previous millenniums.

Angels were hurrying to and fro making final preparations. Errands were being run, and the hosts of heaven were organizing for the forthcoming journey to earth. We, the multitudes of the redeemed, were also being arranged into units to accompany the Father, the Son, and the Holy Spirit, together with the angels as they returned to the earth once again. This, incidentally, would be the third time that Jesus, our leader, would return to the world in a formal way.

On the day of the great event, orders were issued and the trumpets sounded. The heavenly hosts together with the multitudes of the redeemed left the city, accompanying Jesus. The Holy City would follow, not too far behind. The trip, as we now thought of it, was not long. We traveled through the open space of Orion, and continued onward in the direction of the earth.[1] After a relatively short time we looked ahead, and there, first as a small dot, growing larger by the minute as we approached it, was the world in which we had lived.

But what a terrible sight it was! There had been no change since we had seen it a thousand years before. It was one mass of ruins, a site

THE LAST BATTLE

of desolation! The only living things were Satan and his angels. They had been, during the millennium, the only spectators of the disastrous results of their reign, and they were miserable and dejected. But now they could see the descending hosts and knew that what had been prophesied was about to be fulfilled—they would be released for a time.[2]

As we drew near the earth, our host hovered over the area that in olden times had been known as Israel, Palestine, the Holy Land. Far below us we could see the Mount of Olives with the ruins of old Jerusalem. Then, at a given signal, Jesus, our King, accompanied by an escort of angels, proceeded ahead of us. He was clothed with brightness like lightning. He descended upon the Mount of Olives, the same place from which He had ascended after His thirty-three years as a human being on the earth.

As His feet touched the Mount, it parted asunder and became a great plain, stretching out as far as we could see, to the north, to the south, to the east, and to the west.[3] The Mount of Olives and Mount Zion, near it, were in the center. As we looked at the vast area, now prepared for the location of the capital of the universe, we recalled what we had learned of earthly geography, and as we discussed it among ourselves, we observed that the city would be located on an area that, with the throne of God in the center, would cover all of what had been Israel; most of Jordan, Lebanon, and the Sinai Peninsula; parts of Syria, Saudi Arabia, and Egypt; and more than half the Mediterranean Sea east of Cyprus.

Not long afterward a shout went up from the multitude as we turned to gaze upward: "The city! the great city! it is coming down from God out of heaven!"[4] And there it came in all its splendor and glory! John the revelator, who had seen this spectacle three millenniums before, described it thus: "And I John saw the holy city, new Jerusalem, coming down from God out of heaven, prepared as a bride adorned for her husband." As we watched, the city settled down smoothly on the area that had been prepared for it.[5] All of us then entered the city and went to our homes, which were exactly as we had left them. As we visited among ourselves, we recalled another prophecy of John's that had now been fulfilled: "The tabernacle of God is with men, and he will dwell with them, and they shall be his people, and God himself shall be with them, and be their God."[6]

HOME AT LAST!

After a short period of time to get things settled and organized in the new location, the next act in the drama took place. We, along with Jesus and His escorting angels, again sallied forth from the twelve gates of the city, and from a high vantage point looked toward the earth. After a moment Jesus spoke in terrible, fearful majesty, bidding all the wicked, all those who had resisted Him since the time of Cain, to arise. From all the corners of the earth they came forth. Their first sight was Jesus in all His glory, surrounded by His angels and the multitudes of the redeemed.

For the second time those who had crucified Him were resurrected. Again they saw the prints of the nails in His hands and His feet, and where they had thrust the spear into His side.[7] The kings of the earth, the noblemen, the mean and low, the learned and unlearned, all emerged together. All beheld the Son of man. Together with those who had despised and mocked Him, who had put the crown of thorns upon His sacred brow and had smitten Him with the reed, all beheld Him now in all His kingly majesty. Those who spat upon Him in the hour of His trial now turned from His piercing gaze and from the glory of His countenance. They realized that He was the very One whom they had crucified and derided in His expiring agony. And then there arose one long, protracted wail of agony. As the wicked had done one thousand years before, they once more fled from the presence of the King of kings and Lord of lords. All were seeking to hide in the rocks and ruins of the earth, to shield themselves from His terrible glory.[8]

The millions and millions of people who had just risen, numberless as the sands of the sea, presented a tremendous contrast to the multitudes who had been raised one thousand years before. We had been clothed with immortal youth and beauty as we met our Lord. This group, on the other hand, bore the traces of disease, of death, of the curse. They stepped from their graves as they had entered them.[9]

In one sense, however, the appearance of the group raised in the second resurrection was similar to ours at translation. In that vast throng of the wicked were multitudes of the long-lived race that had existed before the Flood—men of lofty stature, more than twice as tall as men five thousand years later. These men of giant intellect had yielded to the control of fallen angels and had devoted all of their skills and knowledge to the exaltation of themselves. Also in that host were men whose wonderful works of art had led the world to idolize their genius. There were kings and generals who had conquered kingdoms and nations, fierce men who had never lost a battle. They were proud, ambitious warriors such as Napoleon, whose approach had made kingdoms tremble. In death these men had experienced no change. As they emerged from their graves they resumed their thinking, maintaining the same enmity to Christ, the same spirit of rebellion against Him. They were actuated by the same desire to conquer that had ruled them when they had died.[10]

With the resurrection of the wicked, Satan was released from his thousand-year confinement, the period in which he had been restricted to the earth and had no one to tempt. Now he was surrounded by this vast array of people. His hopes revived, and he determined not to yield in his great controversy with God. Jesus had reentered the Holy City with us, and the wicked had emerged from their hiding places. As they did so, they saw the majestic figure of Satan before them, surrounded by his lieutenants. Walking back and forth among his subjects, he took immediate advantage of the situation and began his work. Where they had arisen weak and diseased, he now made them strong. He told them that he and his angels were powerful. As proof of his power, he pointed to the countless millions who had been raised, alleging that he had brought them from their graves.[11]

We who were in the city were kept up-to-date by our angelic friends concerning what was going on outside. While the wicked were recovering their strength in the ruins of the earth, we were inside the city beholding its beauty and glory. We trusted in Jesus, our leader, and felt no fear. We were safe, protected by Him who had lost no battles.[12]

We were informed of the powerful speech that Satan made in a successful effort to rally the forces of the newly resurrected under his command. To begin with, he did not announce to his hearers that he was Satan, claiming rather to be the rightful owner of the world, whose inheritance had been unlawfully wrested from him. He presented himself as a redeemer who was about to rescue the millions before and around him from the most cruel tyranny. As the crowds raised their arms in salute and shouted their support, he declared that

HOME AT LAST!

he would lead them against the camp of the saints and take possession of the City of God.[13]

Satan continued his deception by stating that the number of defenders within the city was small and feeble, and that he, with unnumbered millions in support, would develop a plan that would lead to sure victory.[14] Furthermore, he said, he and his angels, having lived in the city for a long time, were familiar with it and knew its vulnerability. He assured his hearers that it could be taken easily.[15]

Satan's deceptive speech was convincing, and the assembled throng was willing to receive his suggestions and do his bidding. With this support he now proceeded to marshal all the armies of the lost under his banner.[16]

First, plans were laid to take possession of the riches and glory of the New Jerusalem. Satan, the commander in chief, consulted with his lieutenants and with the kings and conquerors and mighty men of the past. A plan of battle was drawn up. Lists were made of items necessary for a successful campaign. There were many skillful artisans in that vast throng, and these were assigned to the construction of all kinds of instruments of war,[17] ranging from those known in the earliest periods of earth's history down to the most ingenious weapons developed shortly before the second return of Jesus, such as jet planes and missiles of various types. Military leaders, famed for their success, organized the throngs of warlike men into companies and divisions.[18] All of this took time, but we hardly knew how long, for time now had little significance to us. It could have been a few months, or it may have been even a hundred years.[19]

Preparations were finally completed, and the day for the attack on the Holy City was set by Satan. The order to advance was given, and from all parts of the earth the countless host moved on to the city—an army such as had never been gathered together by earthly conquerors, such as the combined forces of all ages since war had begun on earth could never equal. Satan, the mightiest of warriors, led these military forces, with his angels close by his side. Kings and warriors followed close afterward. Then came the multitudes of fighters in vast companies, each under its appointed leader. We, who had flown to the top of the city walls to observe the scene with Jesus, noticed that the attacking masses were marching over the broken surface of the earth in perfect order, with military precision, toward the city where we were watching.[20]

Gradually the army of the wicked, in battle array, surrounded the city and prepared to lay siege to it. It was obvious that they expected a fierce conflict. Then, during a pause in the tumult outside, we heard the voice of Jesus reassuring us: "Come, ye blessed of my Father, inherit the kingdom prepared for you from the foundation of the world."[21] Speaking with majesty, He added, this time to both us and to those gathered outside the city, "Behold, ye sinners, the reward of the just! And behold, My redeemed, the reward of the wicked!" And then a curse was pronounced on the attackers. At the same time Jesus gave orders that the twelve gates of the city be closed.

As those outside the walls heard these words, they looked upward and saw the multitude, the glorious company of the redeemed, on the walls of the city. And as they witnessed the splendor of their glittering crowns and saw their faces radiant with glory, reflecting the image of Jesus, their courage began to falter. A sense of the treasure and glory that they had lost rushed upon them, and they then came to the full realization that the wages of sin is indeed death. They saw the holy, happy company whom they had despised, clothed with glory while they were outside the city with every mean and abominable thing.[22]

The next-to-last act of the great controversy between Christ and Satan now took place. Christ, surrounded by His angels and the redeemed, appeared high above the city, seated upon a throne set on a burnished-gold foundation. Above the throne was revealed the cross. It was a fearful and glorious scene! In the presence of the assembled inhabitants of earth and heaven the final coronation of the Son of God took place. Then the ultimate sentence upon the wicked was pronounced.

The eyes of Jesus were fixed upon the wicked throng as the books of record were opened. At the same time, above the throne and the cross, there appeared what could be described as a panoramic history of the world, beginning with the scenes of Adam's temptation and fall, and picturing the successive steps taken in the great plan of redemption. Jesus' life, His sufferings, persecution, and death were shown to the now-silent multitude. The scenes of earth's history appeared in faithful reproduction. Satan and his angels would have given anything to stop the presentation, but had no power to halt the

HOME AT LAST!

depiction of their own perfidy. Each individual among the watching sinners was able to single out his own part in the story of evil. Herod, Herodias, Pilate, soldiers, priests, rulers, Nero, Agrippina, papists, pontiffs, pretended fathers of the church, and every person down to the most humble individual could see how he had performed. All were made aware of every sin that they had committed, and now knew exactly how they had lost their way. They recognized God's justice and kneeled down and worshiped the King of kings.[23]

Satan himself seemed paralyzed as he beheld the glory and majesty of Christ. He who once had been a covering cherub remembered from where he had fallen. Now he saw another standing near to the Father, veiling His glory. In the recent coronation he had seen the crown placed upon the head of Christ by an angel of lofty stature and majestic presence, and he knew that that exalted position could have been his. He thought of the home of his innocence and purity that had been his until he indulged in murmuring against God and in envy of Christ. He recalled that he had made no effort for self-recovery when God had offered to grant him forgiveness. He reviewed his work among men and its results. He saw that his wicked plots had been powerless to destroy those who had placed their trust in Jesus. As Satan looked upon his kingdom, he saw only failure and ruin. For the time being, his accusations against the mercy and justice of God were silenced. Now, together with all his angels, he too joined his subjects and bowed down, confessing the justice of his sentence.[24]

This feeling, however, lasted for only a moment. Satan came to himself again, his character still unchanged. The spirit of rebellion, like a mighty torrent, again burst forth. Filled with frenzy, he determined not to yield in the great controversy, and decided on a last desperate struggle against the King of heaven. He rushed into the midst of his kneeling subjects, and endeavored to inspire them with his own fury and rally them to instant battle.

But now, of all the millions whom he had allured into rebellion, there were none to acknowledge his supremacy. His power had come to an end. The wicked were still filled with the same hatred of God that inspired Satan, but they saw that their cases were hopeless, that they could not prevail against the great Jehovah. Their rage was kindled against Satan and against those who had been his agents in deception, and with the fury of demons they turned upon them.[25]

THE LAST BATTLE

It was at this juncture that the final act of judgment was executed. As we watched from the safety of the Holy City, the whole earth surrounding us burst into fire. The earth was broken up, and the coal and oil and fires that God had reserved for the final destruction came into full play. Devouring flames exploded from every yawning chasm. The very rocks were ablaze. The day had come that would burn as an oven. The elements melted with fervent heat. The earth's surface seemed as a molten mass—a vast, seething, boundless lake of liquid fire.[26]

The fire from God rained upon the host of the wicked outside the city. It fell upon the great men, the mighty men, the noble, the poor, and the miserable. They were punished according to the deeds done in the body. Though all were consumed together, all did not perish at the same time. During the judgment held in heaven during the previous thousand years, the saints, together with Jesus, had determined the exact amount of punishment that each should suffer. Some suffered for many days, while others were destroyed quickly. Nevertheless, as long as there was a portion of them unconsumed, all the sense of suffering remained. An angel said, "The worm of life shall not die; their fire shall not be quenched as long as there is the least particle for it to prey upon."

Satan and his angels suffered longer than those whom they had led to perdition. Even after his angels were consumed, Satan still continued to suffer, for he bore the weight and punishment for not only his own sins but also his part in the sins of the redeemed host. He had to suffer for the ruin of souls that he had caused. So, after all had perished, he still lived and suffered on. But finally he also was totally destroyed, consumed by the fire. He, the root, together with his followers, the branches, were no more. All had died the everlasting death. For them there would be no other resurrection. The full penalty of the law had been visited, and the demands of justice had been met. Satan's work of ruin was now forever ended.[27]

In the meantime we, the faithful of all ages, continued within the protection of the walls of the New Jerusalem. Although the entire earth was wrapped in the sea of liquid fire, the area where the city rested was preserved just as the ark had been protected during the Flood. The miracle of God's power kept us unharmed amid the devouring elements. He was to His people both a sun and a shield.[28]

HOME AT LAST!

These were not times of joy for the Holy Trinity, the angels, or for us, the multitude of redeemed. Loved ones and friends were suffering outside the walls that were protecting us. While tears for individuals had been banished more than a thousand years before, there still remained the sadness caused by sin and the resulting eternal destruction of those outside the city. There were heartaches and tears as long as the smoke ascending from the fire could be perceived.

But finally the punishment was completed. The wicked had been burnt up as stubble and had been converted to ashes. It was over![29] It was now, at the end of the great controversy between Christ and Satan, when the victory of heaven was complete, that the angelic host, together with all of the redeemed saints, joined by the inhabitants of the entire loyal universe, cried out in a loud voice of praise and triumph, "Amen![30] It is finished!"

References

[1] *Early Writings*, pp. 41, 291.
[2] Rev. 20:3; *The Great Controversy*, p. 663.
[3] Zech. 14:4; *Spiritual Gifts*, vol. 3, p. 84.
[4] *Early Writings*, p. 291.
[5] Rev. 21:1, 2; *ibid*.
[6] Verse 3; *Education*, p. 302.
[7] *Spiritual Gifts*, vol. 3, pp. 84, 85; *Early Writings*, p. 292.
[8] *Ibid*.
[9] *The Great Controversy*, p. 662; *Spiritual Gifts*, vol. 3, p. 84.
[10] *The Great Controversy*, pp. 662-664; *Early Writings*, p. 293; *The SDA Bible Commentary*, Ellen G. White Comments, on Rev. 20:5, 6, p. 986.
[11] *Early Writings*, p. 293.
[12] *Early Writings*, p. 53.
[13] *The Great Controversy*, p. 663.
[14] *Early Writings*, p. 293; *The Great Controversy*, p. 663.
[15] *Spiritual Gifts*, vol. 3, p. 85.
[16] *The Great Controversy*, p. 663.
[17] *Ibid.*, p. 664; *Early Writings*, p. 294.
[18] *The Great Controversy*, p. 664.
[19] Isa. 65:20.
[20] *Ibid.*; *Early Writings*, pp. 53, 54, 294.
[21] Matt. 25:34; *Early Writings*, p. 53.
[22] *Ibid.*, p. 294.
[23] *The Great Controversy*, pp. 666-669.
[24] *Ibid.*, pp. 669, 670.
[25] *Ibid.*, pp. 671, 672.
[26] Mal. 4:1; 2 Peter 3:10; *The Great Controversy*, pp. 672, 673; *Spiritual Gifts*, vol. 3, pp. 87, 88.
[27] Mal. 4:1; Isa. 34:8; Prov. 11;31; *Early Writings*, pp. 54, 294, 295; *The Great Controversy*, p. 673.
[28] Rev. 20:6; Ps. 84:11; *The Great Controversy*, p. 673; *Spiritual Gifts*, vol. 3, p. 87; *The SDA Bible Commentary*, Ellen G. White Comments, on Rev. 20:9, 10, 14, p. 986.
[29] Mal. 4:1, 3.
[30] *Early Writings*, p. 295; *The Great Controversy*, p. 673.

Chapter Eight

The New Earth

A new phase of eternal life now opened to us. The punishing fire that had consumed the wicked had also purified the earth. Not a single physical sign of the curse remained. The broken, uneven surface of the earth around the New Jerusalem now had the general appearance of a level, extensive plain. The rough, ragged mountains had melted with the fervent heat. Even the atmosphere was cleansed. As all that had to do with the curse of evil was consumed, the fire had died away, the last wisps of smoke had disappeared, and all the results of sin had been converted into ashes. We were pleased to know that there would be no eternally burning hell to keep before us the fearful consequences of sin. Only the scars in the hands and the side of our Saviour would do that![1]

God spoke, and the earth was made new. With unexpressible pleasure we looked upon the country that was our eternal inheritance.[2] God's original purpose in the creation of the earth was now fulfilled, that of providing His children a land that they would inhabit forever, and a city whose Builder and Maker was God.[3] By faith some of the early patriarchs and prophets had seen what we now were seeing, such men as Abraham, who during his life had sought rest in the land promised to him, but finally had to purchase a place to lay his bones;[4] Moses, who led God's people for forty years through the desert, had seen the earthly Canaan from the heights of Mount Nebo, and had, in addition, been given a vision of the earth freed from curse, lovelier than the fair land of promise that spread before him;[5] ill-fated Balaam, who saw the redeemed rejoicing in the unfading glories of the earth made new;[6] and John the Beloved, to whom had been revealed this heavenly city with all its splendor and dazzling glory.[7]

HOME AT LAST!

We entered into this new phase of life with unbounded joy, knowing that the discomforts with which we had lived were gone forever. There would be no more handicapped—no lame, no blind, no deaf. There would nevermore be pain, sickness, or death; no parting, no more funeral trains, no grief, no sorrow, no crying, no dirge of crushed hopes and buried affections. It was now that God's promise was fulfilled, "God shall wipe away all tears from their eyes."[8] Furthermore, we had been told that though we would still have free wills, the situation was such that affliction would never rise up the second time.[9]

We traveled from time to time away from the capital city to become acquainted with other parts of the earth made new. We walked on tree-shaded paths and highways prepared for us by the Lord, and saw that this new world was exceedingly beautiful, with matchless charms. Its surface was diversified with mountains, hills, and plains, interspersed with noble rivers and lovely lakes. It was not one extensive plain, but rather widespread tablelands swelling into hills of beauty, with the mountains of God rearing their lofty summits in the background. The latter were not abrupt and rugged, abounding in terrific steeps and frightful chasms as they had been during the millenniums of earth's previous history. What had been the sharp, ragged bony edges of earth's rocky framework were now regular and beautiful in shape. Bare, high rocks were not seen upon them. There were ever-flowing streams, clear as crystal. The waters were evenly dispersed.[10]

At times we had wondered whether there would be sufficient room for the multitudes of the redeemed. As we traveled from place to place over the surface of the earth, we could see that this was no problem. During our lives on sinful earth we were aware that almost 75 percent of the surface of the globe was made up of salty oceans, with another 5 percent of the land as barren wilderness and deserts, thus leaving only 20 percent of the surface available for habitation. Even at that, more than 4 billion people had been living upon the earth when it came to its tragic end!

The situation was now reversed. There were no more great seas to serve as barriers, no fathomless oceans to divide friends. There were no fierce torrents, no restless, murmuring waves.[11] Now this 75 percent of the earth was available for habitation.

THE NEW EARTH

The barren places were also changed. Water now broke out in the wilderness, and rivulets in the desert. Where before there had been parched ground, we could now see pools and lakes, and there were springs where before had been thirsty land. The waste places had become like the Garden of Eden, and the deserts were beautiful areas planted by the Lord. Reeds, rushes, and tall grass formed a living green carpet that covered the earth.[12]

Everywhere our eyes saw color, both restful and stimulating. Every type of vegetation adorned the hills, mountains, and plains. There were majestic trees of every description waving their green banners. Fir trees had replaced the thorns, and myrtle trees the briars. Straight, lofty trees crowned the tops of hills, trees that far surpassed in size, beauty, and perfect propotion any that we had known on the old earth. We were told by our special angel friends that their wood was of fine grain and hard substance, closely resembling stone, and hardly less enduring. Besides these, there were other trees of every variety to beautify the landscape—the box, the pine, the oil, the pomegranate, and the fig. Many of them were laden with every kind of fruit—good for food, fragrant and delicious, beautiful to the eye and pleasant to the taste. There were woods here and there, not dark and dank as we had known on the earth, but light and glorious.[13]

There were also lovely vines, growing upright, unsupported yet presenting a most graceful appearance, with their branches drooping under their load of tempting fruit. This fruit was large and of many different hues—some nearly black, and others purple, red, pink, and light green. This beautiful and luxuriant growth of fruit upon the branches of the vines was called grapes. Not all vines stood alone. Some were supported by trees. In spite of not being supported by trellises none trailed upon the ground, but the weight of the fruit bowed them down. It would be our happy labor to train these vines.[14]

Aside from the trees and the vines, the hills, mountains, and plains were gemmed with myriads of graceful shrubs and flowers of every variety, description, hue, and color. All were tastefully and gloriously arranged. The fragrance of roses, lilies, and thousands of other flowers pervaded the atmosphere. There was no blight to affect them, and their beauty and fragrance were permanent.[15] The effects of sin that resulted in death were not visible among them. The natural processes of germination, growth, buds, and fruits continued in a

67

HOME AT LAST!

normal way, unimpeded by plagues, insects, droughts, and floods. They were now what God had intended them to be, decorations of beauty for the enjoyment of man. As we walked through all this enchanting panorama, we could see here and there gold, silver, and precious stones strewn about in abundance.[16]

During the years we had spent in the capital city, and now during the time we had already spent on the earth made new, we had noticed that the temperature was even, and the atmosphere was pure and clear. There were no chilling winds, no disagreeable changes. The air was perfectly clean and healthful.[17] Away from the city, at night, as we looked up we could see the starry worlds on high, set there by our loving Father.[18]

Although the sun and the moon existed, they did not have the same function that we had been accustomed to on earth. Their light had no effect upon us either by day or by night, and this in spite of the fact that the sun was seven times stronger and that the moon shone as brightly as the sun had shone formerly. There was no need of artificial lighting such as candles, lamps, light bulbs, and flashlights. The light of the sun, in the New Jerusalem itself, was superseded by a radiance that, though not painfully dazzling, immeasurably surpassed the brightness of the noonday in previous times. It was the glory of the Godhead that flooded the capital city with unfading light. There we walked in the sunless brightness of perpetual day.[19]

Everywhere we went we saw angels and people enjoying these glorious sights. At times we had glimpses of Adam and Eve walking hand in hand together with some of their children and grandchildren. We could hear their remarks of pleasure and satisfaction, particularly as they strolled through the Garden of Eden, which had been their home for a while. Before they were cast out for their disobedience, Adam and Eve had trained the vines, taken care of the trees, eaten the fruit from many of them, and had cared for the flowers. As they went from place to place in the garden, they recognized some of these, and even remembered the names that they had given both trees and flowers for identification purposes. Everything was clothed with heavenly light emanating from the center of the city. As Adam and Eve saw all of this, as they saw the redeemed, their descendants, enjoying it all, they at times would break out in song and praise to God for salvation through Jesus Christ, which had made it possible

THE NEW EARTH

for all of us to be there.[20]

There were some places in the world where we saw all kinds of animals, at times pasturing together in the same field. When Adam and Eve saw the animals, they recognized them as they had the plants, trees, and flowers. They were thoroughly acquainted with their nature and habits, and had named them in accordance with these. Sin had developed fear, hatred, and cruelty in many animals, but now all this was changed. Unlimited control over every living creature had been returned to man. The king of beasts and the lamb played peacefully and harmlessly together or lay down at our feet. We saw lions, sheep, leopards, and wolves all in perfect union, with their offspring. Their natures had been changed, their diet shifted from carnivorous to herbivorous.

At times as we walked through the midst of them they would look at us and then follow on peaceably after us. The fierce had become gentle, and the timid trustful. Ravenous beasts were now nonexistent. Since our arrival from earth more than one thousand years before, little children had loved to play with all of these creatures. There was nothing destructive in the new earth. As we traveled around we saw other animals that we remembered from our days on the old earth, such as goats, cows, bears, oxen, and even reptiles.[21]

Flying through the air were birds of every variety. They flitted among the trees and flowers as we traveled along, while their mellow-toned music echoed among the trees in sweet accord. How happy we were to see them in their bright feathers, warbling their happy, cheerful music. At times we would spontaneously unite with them and raise our voices in harmonious songs of love, praise, and adoration to our Father and our Older Brother, thanking them for the tokens of love that surrounded us.[22]

After exploring, walking, and hiking through nature, we looked forward to returning to our homes in the city. There we lived in the mansions that Christ had prepared for us.[23] Now we were given the opportunity of having a piece of property outside the capital, and of building homes according to our own fancies. God had always intended that our lives would be the same as He had planned for Adam and Eve, lives of activity in the garden and the field. As we had explored the earth in recent times, we had chosen certain locations

HOME AT LAST!

that were then granted to us by the Lord. And there, in the country, we built our own houses.

It was interesting to see the different styles of homes constructed by us and our neighbors. All were beautiful. Some had the appearance of silver. The builders had adorned them with pearls that they had gathered, and the abodes were most glorious to behold. One owner saw us admiring his house and invited us in. As we entered, we could see a golden shelf with a glittering crown on it.[24]

Still other homes were made up of trees and vines. There was no need of protection from the elements, for it was eternal spring. There was no rain. The vegetation received its moisture from the dew or mist, as had been the case before the Flood.[25] My companion and I had opted for a home of this kind. We trained the branches of vines to form bowers, thus making for ourselves a dwelling from living trees covered with foliage, and providing fruit both inside and outside. How pleasant it was to live in a home with the blue heavens as its dome; the earth, with its delicate flowers and grassy carpet of living green as its floor; and the leafy branches of the goodly trees as its canopy. Its walls were hung with the most magnificent adornings, the handiwork of our great Master Artist.

And above all, what thrilled our souls was the knowledge that we would enjoy this home forever. On earth we had built and planted, but too often had not been able to enjoy what we had worked for. Not so now. Now we could build houses and inhabit them. We could plan vineyards and eat the fruit of them. We could now for ever enjoy the work of our hands. We would not labor in vain, nor bring forth for trouble, for we and our children were the blessed of the Lord.[26]

References

[1] *The Great Controversy*, p. 674; *Early Writings*, pp. 53, 54, 179, 295; *Prophets and Kings*, p. 729.
[2] Heb. 11:14-16; Isa. 60:21.
[3] Ps. 37:29; Isa. 45:18; Heb. 11:10; *The Great Controversy*, p. 674.
[4] *Patriarchs and Prophets*, p. 137.
[5] *Ibid.*, p. 477.
[6] *Ibid.*, p. 447.
[7] Rev. 21:10; *Early Writings*, p. 231.
[8] Chaps. 22:1, 4, 5; 21:4; Isa. 11:6, 9; 33:24; 35:5, 6; 62:3; 65:19; *Thoughts From the Mount of Blessing*, p. 17; *The Great Controversy*, pp. 676, 650, 651; *Prophets and Kings*, p. 729; *Testimonies*, vol. 9, p. 287.
[9] Nahum 1:9.
[10] Isa. 35:8; *Patriarchs and Prophets*, p. 44; *The Story of Redemption*, pp. 20, 431; *Testimonies*, vol. 7, p. 76; *The Adventist Home*, p. 542.
[11] Isa. 33:21; Rev. 21:1; *The SDA Bible Commentary*, Ellen G. White Comments, on Rev. 21:1, p. 988.
[12] Isa. 35:6, 7; 51:3; *Prophets and Kings*, p. 729; *Spiritual Gifts*, vol. 2, p. 53; *Early Writings*, p. 18.
[13] *Patriarchs and Prophets*, pp. 47, 90; *My Life Today*, pp. 175, 354; *The Story of Redemption*, p. 21; *Spiritual*

THE NEW EARTH

Gifts, vol. 2, p. 54; *Testimonies*, vol. 1, p. 68; vol. 5, p. 421.

[14] *The Story of Redemption*, pp. 21, 22; *Patriarchs and Prophets*, pp. 47, 90.

[15] *Patriarchs and Prophets*, pp. 44, 90; *My Life Today*, pp. 175, 354; *Testimonies*, vol. 2, p. 258.

[16] *Patriarchs and Prophets*, p. 90.

[17] *Ibid.*, p. 44; *My Life Today*, p. 354.

[18] *Patriarchs and Prophets*, p. 45.

[19] Isa. 30:26; 60:19, 20; Rev. 22:5; 21:23, 25; *The Great Controversy*, p. 676; *The Ministry of Healing*, pp. 504-507; *Maranatha*, p. 358; *Prophets and Kings*, p. 730.

[20] *The Adventist Home*, p. 541; *The Great Controversy*, pp. 647, 648; *Spiritual Gifts*, vol. 3, p. 89.

[21] Isa. 11:6-9; 35:9; *Spiritual Gifts*, vol. 2, pp. 53, 55; *Education*, p. 304; *My Life Today*, p. 354; *Patriarchs and Prophets*, pp. 45, 46, 51; *The Story of Redemption*, pp. 22, 23; *Counsels on Diet and Foods*, p. 396.

[22] *The Story of Redemption*, pp. 22, 23.

[23] John 14:2.

[24] *Early Writings*, p. 18.

[25] Gen. 2:5, 6; *Patriarchs and Prophets*, pp. 96, 97.

[26] Isa. 65:21-23; *Patriarchs and Prophets*, pp. 47, 49; *Education*, p. 304; *Spiritual Gifts*, vol. 2, p. 53.

Chapter Nine

We, the People

We were now more than one thousand years old and had almost reached the physical growth that God had planned for mankind several millenniums before. At the time of the resurrection and the translation when Jesus had come to earth for the second time, we had differed greatly in size and appearance. All had come out of the graves with the same stature as when they had been buried. Adam was of lofty height and majestic form, in stature just a bit shorter than the Son of God. He presented a marked contrast to those of us who had appeared on the scene of action in subsequent generations.

But all had arisen or been transformed exhibiting the freshness and vigor of youth. All blemishes and deformities had been left in the grave.[1] Our bodies had been restored to their original perfection, and were in the spotless image of Jesus.[2] In spite of this, we could recognize others, and they could recognize us.[3] Our features were perfect and beautiful, yet our personal identities had been preserved.[4] During the more than one thousand years since we had left the old earth we had free access to the tree of life. As a result we had gradually grown up to the originally planned stature of our race in its primeval glory. Now there remained no traces of the curse of sin, and we appeared in the beauty of our Lord, in mind and soul and body reflecting His perfect image.[5]

It had taken some time to adjust to the fact that we were growing physically. But as the years passed we men eventually attained the height of Adam, the father of the human race. According to the ancient earth measure we were now around fifteen feet tall (4.6 meters), more than twice the height we previously had been. The women were around twelve feet (3.7 meters) tall, their heads reaching a little above the men's shoulders. We were all symmetrical and well-proportioned, and the women were of noble bearing and very beautiful.[6]

Along with our physical growth there had been an increase in vigor. Our vital force became twenty times as much as we had had previously.[7] There had also been mental development. After the resurrection we had been endowed with a higher nature.[8] We were now upright, with noble traits of character, and no bias toward evil. We had been gifted with high intellectual powers.[9] God had granted us great wisdom and skill, and these could be increased through exercise.[10] We were now completely in harmony with the will of God, and could easily comprehend divine mysteries. Our affections were pure, our appetites and passions were under the control of reason. We were holy and happy in bearing the image of our God, and were in perfect obedience to His will.[11] And yet we were still free moral agents with full liberty to yield or withhold obedience.[12]

We wore no artificial garments. Rather we were covered with white robes, garments of light and glory the same as the angels wore, and we moved about enshrouded in this celestial covering. In addition we, as well as our children, now had wings and made good use of them.[13]

God had given us rest from trials, but we were always occupied, always working, always traveling, always studying. We carried out the will of God and praised His name continually. Yet we never became weary. We alway felt the freshness of morning and were far from its close.[14]

And the children—what a pleasure it was to see them. Now there was no strife or discord among them. Their love was fervent and holy, and their countenances beamed with joy, expressive of their perfect freedom and happiness.[15] Some children had a border of red on their garments of light, an indication that they had participated in the earthly martyrdom of their parents, who also wore a red border around their shining robes.[16] All the children at times could be seen wearing the crowns and carrying the harps that had been given them at the time of Jesus' second coming.[17]

There had been no marriages and no children born during the thousand years we spent in heaven, and neither would there be any on the new earth.[18] God's purpose in making Adam and Eve fruitful, that of multiplying and replenishing the earth, had been fulfilled. The

HOME AT LAST!

billions of redeemed were occupying the earth, and it was now fully inhabited.[19] Yet the loves and sympathies God had implanted in our hearts found truest and sweetest expression.[20]

We rejoiced in the benefits bestowed upon us, and in our powerful minds. Certain things that had seemed so important to us in the past now had virtually lost their significance in our memories. At times, after our arrival in heaven, friends and loved ones who had preceded us in death had asked about events that had taken place while they were resting. But no matter how we tried, no matter how we endeavored to call up earth's greatest trials, we were not able to do so. The exceeding and eternal weight of glory that surrounded us in the new earth made our sufferings seem so trivial that we just could not speak about them.[21]

The only reminder that remained of earthly trials was Jesus Himself. He still bore, and would forever bear, the marks of the price paid for our redemption, the marks of His crucifixion. Upon His wounded head, upon His side, hands, and feet, were the only traces of the cruel work that sin had wrought. And these tokens of His humiliation were His highest honor. That He, our Creator, should humiliate Himself for love to us ever excited our wonder and adoration. Through the eternal ages the wounds of Calvary were to show forth His praise and declare His power.[22]

References

[1] *The Great Controversy*, p. 644.
[2] *Education*, p. 309; *My Life Today*, p. 153.
[3] 1 Cor. 13:12; *Education*, p. 306; *The Desire of Ages*, p. 804; *The Great Controversy*, p. 677; Letter 79, 1898.
[4] *The SDA Bible Commentary*, Ellen G. White Comments, on 1 Cor. 15:42-52, p. 1093; *The Story of Redemption*, p. 21.
[5] *The Great Controversy*, p. 645.
[6] Mal. 4:2; *Spiritual Gifts*, vol. 3, p. 84; *The Story of Redemption*, p. 21.
[7] *Testimonies*, vol. 3, pp. 138, 139.
[8] Manuscript 36, 1906.
[9] *Patriarchs and Prophets*, pp. 49, 50.
[10] *Education*, p. 15; *Patriarchs and Prophets*, p. 90.
[11] *Patriarchs and Prophets*, p. 45.
[12] Ibid., p. 49.
[13] Isa. 40:31; *Spiritual Gifts*, vol. 2, p. 54; *Early Writings*, p. 54; *The Great Controversy*, p. 677.
[14] Verse 31; *The Great Controversy*, pp. 676, 677; *"That I May Know Him"*, p. 371.
[15] *My Life Today*, p. 357.
[16] *Spiritual Gifts*, vol. 2, p. 54; *Early Writings*, pp. 18, 19.
[17] *My Life Today*, p. 357.
[18] *Selected Messages*, book 1, pp. 172, 173; book 2, p. 25; Letter 59, 1904; Matt. 22:30.
[19] Gen. 1:28; Isa. 45:18.
[20] *The Great Controversy*, p. 677.
[21] *Early Writings*, p. 17; *My Life Today*, p. 357.
[22] Hab. 3:4, margin; *The Great Controversy*, pp. 651, 674.

Chapter Ten

Always Busy

Many, many years before, some of us had had the mistaken idea that heaven would be a place where all the redeemed would do was play their harps, sing, and go to religious services. The time in between would be spent in a do-nothing state of dreamy idleness. Some dreaded such a life. We were happy, however, to discover that this was not the case. While it was true that the word *rest* was definitely applicable, it was not physical rest, but a glorious rest to the weary and heavy laden, an eternal rest from warring against sin and the temptations of Satan.

The new earth actually was a place of productive and interesting activity. Work was carried on constantly. The economy provided no place for idlers. The angels, and even God the Father, God the Son, and God the Holy Spirit were always busy. None, however, considered this intense activity wearing or burdensome, but felt that it was part of the program of rest. The family of the redeemed found their delight in serving Him whose they were by creation and redemption.[1]

None of this activity, however, was self-centered. Everything done was noble and elevated. It was the chief pleasure of all to witness and add to the joy and happiness of those around them. Rest was found in loving service to others. No worldly business leading to the accumulation of money, of property, to the aggrandizement of the individual was to be found.[2]

A part of our time was set aside for physical labor, the kind of activity that brought satisfaction to Adam and Eve in the first Garden of Eden—work in the garden and in the field. This had again become a pleasure, for the curse brought on by sin had been removed. There were no more weeds, no pests, no droughts, no floods. God in His

HOME AT LAST!

great love had already planted gardens for us. A portion of our time was dedicated to the happy employment of dressing these, and this labor was not tiresome but pleasant and invigorating. This was particularly so since we knew that this was our eternal home and that we would always be able to enjoy that which we had planted.[3]

But life on the new earth was not confined solely to work. There were many other enjoyable things to do! Much of our time was spent in communion with others. Harmonious social life with the blessed angels, with the princes of God, and with the faithful ones of all ages; the sacred fellowship that bound us together as God's family was among the experiences that we truly enjoyed. We were a happy family, clothed with the garments of praise and thanksgiving. How great was our joy as we met in unity! And the greatest of all thrills was the association with Christ on terms of freedom and equality.[4]

At one time or another, all of us visited other worlds, worlds that had never sinned, that had always been obedient to the law of God.[5] Now, unfettered by mortality, unlimited by time, we flew afar without becoming tired. Among the worlds that we visited was one that seemed very bright and glorious. The grass there was a living green, and birds warbled sweet songs. The inhabitants were noble, majestic, and lovely. They, like us, bore the express image of Jesus, and their countenances beamed with holy joy, expressive of the freedom and happiness of the place. When Ellen White saw that world in vision many years before, it, like our own first Garden of Eden, had two trees, one of which looked much like the tree of life in the New Jerusalem. Then there was a second tree, of which they had been told not to eat. Though the fruit on both trees was very beautiful, the people had only eaten of the first one, but had never tasted of the second. They had been obedient to the command with which our own race had failed to comply. Another of the worlds that we visited had seven moons.[6]

All of this travel opened to our minds realities that we had not understood while on the old sin-cursed earth. We had known that inhabitants of other planets had sung and shouted for joy when Christ created our world.[7] But somehow many of us had not fully grasped this and had had the idea that our own world and the heavenly mansions constituted the main part of the universe of God. Now, as we ranged afar, we discovered that this was not so. We learned that there were millions of inhabited worlds,[8] and that our own planet was but an atom in the universe.[9] And yet it was on this little speck of earth that God had placed the human family, individuals that among all created beings were the noblest, ranking just below the angels themselves.[10] And it was this world that had attracted the attention of every eye in the universe when its inhabitants had disregarded God's law, making it the only blot in God's perfect creation. The other worlds had been filled with sorrow at the spectacle of human woe, and rang with songs of gladness at the tidings of a ransomed soul.

Sometimes ministering angels had visited the earth to provide aid. Time after time these heavenly intelligences had led armies. They had helped eliminate pestilence. They had eaten at the humble board of poor families, and often had appeared as weary travelers in need of shelter for the night.[11] As we now visited them and told them of our own experience, these holy beings saw the price that had been paid for our redemption, and they were filled with amazement.[12]

Our world was the one honored above all others because its Creator, the Lord Jesus, had been willing to humble Himself, even to the death of the cross, in order to redeem His created beings. Now this world had been selected to hold the capital of the universe! Here God had come to make His home among the ransomed race.[13]

Now, as we visited other worlds, with unutterable delight we entered the joy and the wisdom of the unfallen beings. We searched out the mysteries of redemption, and rejoiced as the holy ones shared with us the treasures of knowledge and understanding gained through ages upon ages in contemplation of God's handiwork. With undimmed vision we now gazed upon the glories of creation—suns and stars and systems, all in their appointed order circling the throne of God.[14]

All of this, of course, was part of and directly related to the process that would be an eternal one—our education! We came to realize more and more that the training that we had received on earth had been only a beginning, that it would continue throughout all eternity, ever progressing, never completed. We found that every right principle and every truth that we had learned in earthly schools advanced us in this heavenly school. The education we had begun on earth was now being perfected. We had only entered a higher grade.[15]

HOME AT LAST!

The central school was heaven, an open school. The curriculum was the universe. Our main teacher was Jesus Himself. A branch of this school had first been established in the original Garden of Eden, and now that the plan of redemption had been accomplished, that system of education had been reimplanted in the Eden restored.[16]

The 144,000 were particularly favored, for they were privileged to go with Jesus wherever He went.[17] Christ, aided by the angels, also accompanied different groups of us on various occasions, even as He had led His disciples during the three and one-half years He had been on earth, and He imparted rich stores of knowledge in many things. Instruction was face to face and heart to heart.

The science of all sciences, basic to all else, was the study of the plan of redemption. We found sources for this study in the capital, in the rest of the new earth, and in other worlds. This study included the love of God the Father, which led Him to give up His only Son; the love of Christ, which had led to His incarnation, His humiliation, His atoning sacrifice, and His mediatorial work. This study, we were told, would employ our minds throughout eternity. We contemplated with never-failing delight the wonders of creative power, the mysteries of redeeming love.

We were not the only ones who participated in this study. It had engaged the attention of the angels and of all the intelligences of the unfallen worlds. How true it was that this was the highest study in which we could participate, and that it quickened our minds and uplifted our souls. Furthermore, there was no limit to its possibilities.[18] From this school of Christ we would never graduate. Since God is infinite, and in Him are all treasures of wisdom, we would throughout eternity be ever searching, ever learning, yet would never exhaust the riches of His wisdom, His goodness, or His power. As we continued in these studies, new views of the perfection and glory of Christ appeared. The cross of Christ was our science and our song. We found ourselves to be constantly advancing in wisdom, refinement, and nobility of soul as new and rich developments were made manifest in the plan of salvation. Every one of our powers was developed, and every capability increased. Our energies were never exhausted, nor did our minds ever become weary.[19]

There were some among the redeemed who had never quite understood the elementary facts of the plan of salvation. Others had laid hold of Christ in the last hours of their life and had little knowledge of Him. Special classes were held in order to open to these the things they had not been able to assimilate while on earth.[20] The fact is that there were many points that had perplexed all of us while we were on the old earth. There had been matters concerning which God had kept silent because of the limitations of our human minds that hindered us in gathering up and appreciating that which had been made known. Now the ways of Providence were clear; the mysteries of grace through Christ were unfolded. Actually, we now saw that the record of the lives of the redeemed had been a series of uninterrupted victories, although at the time it had not seemed so.[21] Now that which our minds had not been able to grasp, that which had appeared to us as confusion and broken promises, that which had been hard to understand, was explained. Now we saw order in what had seemed unexplainable; wisdom in what had been withheld; goodness and gracious mercy in everything imparted. We realized that infinite love had ordered the experiences that to us had seemed most trying. Truth was now unfolded to our minds, free from obscurity, frankly and directly, and its brightness was endurable. Controversies were ended and all difficulties were solved, and our hearts sang for joy.[22]

One facet of study that helped us to understand better God's great love was that which had to do with nature. All the treasures of the universe were now opened to us. We shared the treasures to be gained through ages upon ages in contemplation of God's handiwork. We were studying the secrets of the laboratory of nature. We saw how all creation, in its surpassing loveliness, offered to God a constant tribute of praise and adoration. And as time went on, more and more glorious revelations were made manifest.[23]

A vast field of study in astronomy was opened to us as we looked up into the star-studded heavens, and as we traveled through innumerable worlds in their orderly revolutions. All now appeared in the glory and beauty of our Lord and God. We studied the balancing of the clouds, the mysteries of light and sound, of day and night, and the solemn glories of the moon. In every shining star we found God's name, that is, His character of love, written.[24]

We found themes for study in the simple leaves of the forest trees, the spires of grass covering the earth with their green velvet carpet, the plants, the flowers tinted by the Master Artist, the stately trees of

HOME AT LAST!

the forest, the lofty mountains. The laws and operations of nature were opened to our minds by the infinite Framer and Upholder of all. We held converse with leaf and flower and tree, gathering from each the secrets of its life. We became familiar with every living creature, from the mightiest animal that played in the waters to the tiniest mote that floated in the sunbeams. And in everything in the heavens above and the earth beneath, whether a leaf of the forest or a stone of the mountains, as well as in every shining star, we found the Creator's name inscribed. Our every nerve and sense responded joyfully to the expression of God's love in His marvelous works.[25]

Students of science, as well as those of us who had not examined that field on earth, now could read the records of creation. We discovered no reminders of the law of evil. We listened to the music of nature's voices and detected no note of wailing or undertone of sorrow. We beheld the world of beauty that before we had only seen through microscopes, and, as always, in all of the vast universe we could behold God's name written large.[26]

Historians were happy with the sources that were of infinite scope and of wealth inexpressible. On earth, from the vantage ground of God's Word, these scholars had been afforded a minute view of the vast field of history, and had gained some knowledge of the principles that governed the course of human events, but their vision had been clouded, and their knowledge incomplete. Now they were able to see all things clearly. To them was opened the course of the great conflict, the story of sin that had begun before Creation and that had ended with the creation of the new earth. The history of sin now stood as a witness to the fact that with the existence of God's law was bound the happiness of all the beings He had created.

The veil that interposed between the visible and invisible world was now drawn aside, and wonderful things were revealed as historians perused the records. Now they were able to discern the providences of God and were able to understand what man owed to the care and interposition of God's angels—how celestial beings had taken an active part in the affairs of men and thwarted the spoiler's purpose and turned aside the stroke of the destroyer. Though the rulers of the old world had not known it, angels had often been spokesmen in their councils. They had sponsored the cause of the persecuted and oppressed. They had defeated purposes and arrested evils that would have brought wrong and suffering to God's children. To behold in history the outworking and success of true principles was one of the studies and rewards of this heavenly school.[27]

As our minds expanded, we came to the realization that there were no limitations to that which we might do. Eternity gave us the opportunity to carry forward the grandest enterprises, reach the highest aspirations, and realize our loftiest ambitions. And ever before us there were new heights to surmount, new wonders to admire, new truths to comprehend, and fresh objects to call forth the powers of body and mind and soul. New truths were constantly unfolded to our wondering and delighted minds. And the knowledge that through ceaseless ages we would continue to advance in wisdom, in knowledge, and in holiness, ever exploring new fields of thought, ever finding new marvels and new glories, and knowing that there were still beyond us joy and love and wisdom infinite, was at once overwhelming and thrilling. As the years of eternity rolled on, they brought richer and more glorious revelations of God the Father and of Christ the Son. Our love, reverence, and happiness increased. The more we learned about God, the greater was our admiration of His character.[28]

References

[1] John 5:17; *Maranatha*, p. 350; *My Life Today*, p. 358.
[2] *My Life Today*, p. 359; *The SDA Bible Commentary*, Ellen G. White Comments, on Prov. 31:26, 27, p. 1164; *Testimonies*, vol. 5, pp. 276, 280.
[3] Isa. 65:21, 22; *The Story of Redemption*, p. 21; *Prophets and Kings*, p. 730; *Early Writings*, p. 18.
[4] *Testimonies*, vol. 8, p. 42; *Prophets and Kings*, p. 732; *Fundamentals of Christian Education*, pp. 234, 235; *Education*, p. 306; *The Great Controversy*, p. 677.
[5] *Early Writings*, p. 40; *The SDA Bible Commentary*, Ellen G. White Comments, on Rev. 22:14, p. 990.
[6] *Early Writings*, pp. 39, 40.
[7] Job 38:7.
[8] Ellen G. White, in *Signs of the Times*, June 27, 1895; Ellen G. White, in *Review and Herald*, March 1, 1881.
[9] Ellen G. White, in *Review and Herald*, Sept. 29, 1891.
[10] Heb. 2:7; *ibid.*, Dec. 3, 1908.
[11] *Sons and Daughters of God*, p. 37.
[12] *Maranatha*, p. 368.
[13] Rev. 21:3; Ellen G. White, in *Review and Herald*, Sept. 29, 1891; Feb. 25, 1915.
[14] *The Great Controversy*, p. 677; *The SDA Bible Commentary*, Ellen G. White Comments, on Rev. 22:14, p. 990.
[15] *The Ministry of Healing*, p. 466; *Testimonies*, vol. 5, p. 301; *Counsels to Parents and Teachers*, pp. 208, 209; *My Life Today*, p. 161.
[16] *Education*, p. 301.
[17] Rev. 14:4.
[18] 1 Peter 1:12; *My Life Today*, p. 360; *The SDA Bible Commentary*, Ellen G. White Comments, on Rev. 22:14, p. 990; *The Great Controversy*, pp. 651, 677.
[19] *My Life Today*, pp. 360, 361; *The Great Controversy*, pp. 651, 677; *Selected Messages*, book 1, p. 403; *Education*, p. 307; *Testimonies*, vol. 5, pp. 702, 703.
[20] *Selected Messages*, book 1, p. 262.

HOME AT LAST!

[21] *The Desire of Ages*, p. 679; *The SDA Bible Commentary*, Ellen G. White Comments, on 1 Cor. 13:12, p. 1091.
[22] *The SDA Bible Commentary*, Ellen G. White Comments, on 1 Cor. 13:12, p. 1091; *Counsels to Parents and Teachers*, pp. 208, 209; *Maranatha*, p. 321; *Testimonies*, vol. 9, p. 286.
[23] Eph. 3:20; *Testimonies*, vol. 8, p. 42; *Education*, p. 307; *The Great Controversy*, p. 589.
[24] Ps. 19:1; 90:17; Job 37:16; *Patriarchs and Prophets*, p. 51; *The Adventist Home*, p. 548.
[25] *Patriarchs and Prophets*, p. 50, 51; *Testimonies*, vol. 4, p. 581; *My Life Today*, p. 342.
[26] *Education*, p. 303; *The Adventist Home*, p. 547.
[27] *Education*, pp. 304-306.
[28] *Ibid.*, p. 307; *The Great Controversy*, pp. 677, 678; *Testimonies*, vol. 5, p. 703; *Counsels to Parents and Teachers*, p. 55.

Chapter Eleven

Worship

Permeating all of God's universe, spreading through the millions of inhabited worlds and throughout our own world, was the spirit of worship and thankfulness. All nature in its surpassing loveliness offered to God a tribute of praise and adoration. Year after year moved on in gladness. Over the scene the morning stars sang together, and the sons of God shouted for joy, realizing that now there would be no more sin, and neither would there be any more death.[1]

During the years that we had already been in heaven and on the new earth, our own lives and experiences were witnesses to the love, to the greatness, of the Godhead, and this would continue throughout all eternity. It was in witnessing and in service to others that we found our greatest joy, ever telling of the riches of the glory of this mystery—Christ in us who had been our hope of glory.[2]

Now we were able to commune with God directly, with no obscuring veil between. Now we could thank, praise, and worship Him face to face. Now we could receive the tangible visits of the angels.[3] It was no wonder that we were happy!

While the spirit of worship, of praise and adoration, was an integral part of everything that we did, filling every moment of every day of the week, and being felt in every part of the universe, there still were certain occasions when all activity was focused on it to the exclusion of all other activities. Once a month, at the time of the new moon, all creation gathered before the Lord.[4]

And above all there was the weekly Sabbath day. The seventh-day Sabbath had been committed to Adam, father and representative of the entire human family, in the first Garden of Eden. Its observance was to be an act of grateful acknowledgment on the part of all who lived on the earth that God was their Creator and their rightful

Sovereign; that they were the work of His hands and the subjects of His authority. It had been wholly commemorative and had been given to all mankind. And it was to continue as a sign of the Creator's power as long as the heavens and the earth endured.[5]

Now all things had been restored. Eden had bloomed again on earth. We were abiding in the mansions that Christ had prepared for us. God's holy rest day was now honored by all the inhabitants of the universe and was a time of rest and rejoicing. Heaven and the glorified new earth were united in praise as from one week to another the nations of the saved bowed in joyful worship to God and the Lamb.[6]

God's plan for what the Sabbath should be was now fulfilled. He had designed that it would direct our minds to the contemplation of His created works. He wanted us to listen as nature spoke to our senses, declaring that there is a living God, the Creator, the Supreme Ruler of all. He wanted us to see this in the everlasting hills, in the lofty trees, in the opening buds and the delicate flowers, all speaking to us of Him. The Sabbath, ever pointing to Him who made us all, bade us open this great book of nature and trace therein the wisdom, the power, and the love of the Creator.[7]

To speak of worship and to speak of music, of song, is to speak of the same thing. We realized that music formed a definite part of God's worship in His capital, and the statement "Singing, as a part of religious service, is as much an act of worship as is prayer" took on a new meaning in the new earth. There were strains of enrapturing music and song that, save in the visions of God, none of us had heard or even imagined while on the earth. It was melodious, perfect, and entrancing.[8]

This had been so at the time of Creation, when the morning stars had sung together and all the sons of God had shouted for joy, a scene that had been repeated when the earth was purified and renewed and sin destroyed forever.[9]

As we had journeyed from the old earth heavenward, with columns of angels on both sides, there had been song. Harps had been given us, and when the commanding angels first struck the keynote, every voice had been raised in grateful, happy praise, and every hand had skillfully swept over the strings of the harps, sending forth melodious music in rich and perfect strains: "Worthy, worthy is the Lamb that was slain, and hath redeemed us to God by His own most

WORSHIP

precious blood!" There were no select singers or musicians. All of us participated, singing loud hosannas as we waved the palm branches of victory.[10]

And then, when we had arrived in the Holy City, there had been that great gathering as we stood on the crystal sea before God's throne. First all stood in silence and awe as they listened to a new song sung by the special group of 144,000 redeemed, a song of unique deliverance that none other, not even the cherubim and seraphim, could sing. The sound was as of many waters and as the sound of a great thunder. As they sang they accompanied themselves with their harps. This was a song of liberation, the song of Moses and the Lamb. It was a song of experience, an experience such as no other company had ever had. Part of it included the words "Great and marvellous are thy works, Lord God Almighty; just and true are thy ways, thou King of saints. Who shall not fear thee, O Lord, and glorify thy name? for thou only art holy."[11] As we listened, there was no envy or resentment in any heart for not being included in that choir. All rejoiced as they listened to music such as ear had never heard.

Then the millions of redeemed amid the waving of palm branches poured forth a song of praise, a grand finale—clear, sweet, and harmonious. Every voice had joined in this until the anthem swelled through the vaults of heaven, "Salvation to our God which sitteth upon the throne, and unto the Lamb." At this juncture all of the inhabitants of the universe had responded with a profound "Amen." Then the vast host continued, "Blessing, and glory, and wisdom, and thanksgiving, and honour, and power, and might, be unto our God for ever and ever. Amen."[12]

As time swept onward we, the ransomed of the Lord, continued in our praise to God with songs, with words, with our lives. Everlasting joy was on our heads. We had obtained joy and gladness, and sorrow and sighing had fled away. And we expressed this joy and gladness in thanksgiving and the voice of melody, both in song and in playing on instruments.[13]

At times we had gone to the large square surrounding God's throne in the New Jerusalem, and heard special programs presented by the heavenly choirs. As we watched and listened we could see companies of angels standing in a hollow square, each angel with a harp of gold. We could see that at each end of the harp was an

HOME AT LAST!

instrument that could be turned to set the harp or change the key. The angels did not sweep their fingers over the strings carelessly, but touched different strings to produce different sounds. One angel stood above the others and directed the ensemble. He first gave the key by striking a note, and then all would join in rich, perfect melody. They sang enchanting music in melodious strains rising in honor of God and the Lamb, music that was heavenly and divine. As they did, their countenances beamed the image of Jesus, shining with glory unspeakable. As we returned to our homes after such programs, our hearts felt drawn closer to God, and as we carried out our duties, we would sing or hum the keynotes of praise that we had heard.[14]

Some songs that we had sung on the old earth were modified or forgotten, since the circumstances that had motivated them were changed. For example, there were no songs about trouble or crying to God for help; no hymns written from the depths of conscious guilt and self-condemnation; no laments about fleeting breath or closing the eyes in death; no tunes expressing the profound desire for the return of the Lord Jesus. Since the cross of Christ was our perennial song, we did remember such a song as "I love that old cross where the dearest and best for a world of lost sinners was slain." We had not forgotten "Redeemed! how I love to proclaim it! Redeemed by the blood of the Lamb; Redeemed through His infinite mercy, His child, and forever, I am."[15]

And, of course, we could sing with the greatest of pleasure, "There are glories untold in this city of gold. . . . How glorious it is to see Jesus." Ofttimes we could hear Handel's "Hallelujah Chorus" being intoned by some group or other.

Truly we could say that the supreme activity was worshiping our God and our Redeemer, speaking and singing words of praise, thanksgiving, and adoration, and bowing before our Lord in the beauty of holiness.[16]

References

[1] Rev. 21:4; *The Ministry of Healing*, pp. 504-507.
[2] Isa. 43:12; Col. 1:27; *Education*, pp. 308, 309.
[3] *Patriarchs and Prophets*, p. 50.
[4] Isa. 66:23.
[5] Gen. 2:2, 3; Mark 2:27, 28; Matt. 5:18; *Patriarchs and Prophets*, p. 48; *The Desire of Ages*, p. 283.
[6] *Ibid.*, pp. 283, 770.
[7] *Patriarchs and Prophets*, p. 48.
[8] *Education*, p. 161; *Patriarchs and Prophets*, p. 594; *Life Sketches*, p. 172; *Prophets and Kings*, p. 730; *The*

WORSHIP

Great Controversy, p. 542.
[9] Job 38:7; *Education*, p. 161; *Prophets and Kings*, pp. 732, 733.
[10] *Early Writings*, p. 288; *In Heavenly Places*, p. 371; *The Great Controversy*, pp. 651, 652; *The SDA Bible Commentary*, Ellen G. White Comments, on Rev. 15:2, 3; p. 982.
[11] Rev. 7:14; 14:1-4; 15:3, 4; *The Great Controversy*, pp. 648, 649.
[12] Chap. 7:10, 12; *Education*, pp. 308, 309; *The Great Controversy*, pp. 650, 651.
[13] Isa. 35:10; 51:3; 24:14; Ps. 87:7; *Prophets and Kings*, p. 730.
[14] *Testimonies*, vol. 1, p. 146; vol. 2, p. 266; *Education*, p. 168.
[15] Ruth Jaeger Buntain, "The Songs We Will Sing in Heaven," *Adventist Review*, April 23, 1981.
[16] Ps. 29:2.

Chapter Twelve

On Becoming a Citizen

Just how may we gain the privilege of becoming a citizen of this heavenly land, of living in beautiful mansions in the New Jerusalem, of participating in all of those joys?

Life on earth is the beginning of the life in heaven; education on earth is an initiation into the principles of heaven, an education that will enable us to live with God through the eternal ages; lifework here is a training for the lifework there. What we now are, in character and holy service, is the sure foreshadowing of what we shall be. Our preparation for the future world depends upon the way we discharge our duties now in this world. Heaven's communion begins on this earth. It is here that we learn the keynote of its praise. If we wish to enjoy heavenly society in the earth made new, we must be governed by heavenly principles here.[1]

Because of this we must always bear in mind the fact that we are building for eternity. Therefore we must build firmly, on a sure foundation, with persistent effort, to make sure that our house will stand unshaken when storms assail it. This sure foundation is the Rock, Christ Jesus. It is upon Him that we must build for eternity. Paul and Silas expressed it thus: "Believe on the Lord Jesus Christ, and thou shalt be saved."[2] We must carry on a thorough work of grace in our hearts in order to bring our wills into conformity to the mind and will of Christ. We must be able to say, "I am crucified with Christ: nevertheless I live; yet not I, but Christ liveth in me: and the life which I now live in the flesh I live by faith of the Son of God, who loved me, and gave himself for me."[3]

When we submit ourselves freely and completely to Christ, He blends our wills to the will of God and brings about a change in our lives that will prepare us to pass through the pearly gates of the City of

God. We will win in the contest against appetite and every worldly lust. The soul that lives for God, and obeys His Word, unmoved by censure, unperverted by applause, will then abide forever with Him. The city with its foundations of precious stones will receive those who learned while on earth to lean on God for guidance and wisdom, for comfort and hope amid loss and affliction. The songs of angels will welcome them there, and for them the tree of life will yield its fruits.[4]

We need to study the working out of God's purpose in the control of this world to be able to estimate at their true value things both seen and unseen, so that, in viewing the things of time in the light of eternity, we may put them to their truest and noblest use. Thus, learning here the principles of His kingdom and becoming its subjects and citizens, we may be prepared at His coming to enter with Him into its possession. Actually, for the lessons to be learned, the work to be done, the transformation of character to be effected, the time remaining is all too brief a span.[5]

The very atmosphere of heaven is purity, and if we wish to enjoy that place, we must educate and discipline our minds to love purity. We must know the language of heaven and prepare ourselves to sing its song and delight in its spiritual exercises. We must encourage a love for spiritual things. We must make earnest, persistent efforts toward this end, and then we must maintain our faith until the end.[6] If we are truly seeking for eternal riches, we should be striving for the heavenly treasure with far greater earnestness and perseverance, and with an intensity that is proportionate to the value of the object of which we are in pursuit. We should view an eternity of bliss worth a life of persevering and untiring effort. We will set our affections upon things above.[7]

Those of us who are overcomers will receive our reward, the crown of life, and will eat of the tree of life, which is in the midst of the paradise of God.[8] On those beautiful plains, beside those living streams, in those large and pleasant places, we, who were so long pilgrims and wanderers, will find a home. Then, throughout the ceaseless ages of eternity, we shall enjoy with Christ all the glories of the world made new. There will be nothing to disturb or annoy—no sin, no distracting care, nothing to mar our peace. We will enjoy a life of happiness and tranquillity, a life of love and beauty. Our lives will run parallel to the life of Jehovah. To dwell forever in that home of the

HOME AT LAST!

blest, to bear in soul, body, and spirit the perfect likeness of our Creator, and through ceaseless ages to advance in wisdom, in knowledge, ever increasing in capacity to know and to enjoy and to love, and knowing that there is still beyond us joy and love and wisdom infinite—what a glory it will be![9]

When the earth is made new, the great controversy will have ended. Sin and sinners will be no more. The entire universe will be clean. One pulse of harmony and gladness will beat through the vast creation. From the minutest atom to the greatest world we, together with all things, animate and inanimate, in their unshadowed beauty and perfect joy, will declare that God is love.[10] The beautiful new earth, with all its glory, will be our eternal inheritance to possess forever, even forever and ever.[11] The promise made through Zephaniah will have been fulfilled, "At that time I will gather you; at that time I will bring you home."[12]

Jesus said, "Surely I come quickly," and with John the revelator, with deep-felt emotion, we answer, "Even so, come, Lord Jesus."[13]

References

[1] *Education*, pp. 307, 168; *My Life Today*, p. 361; *Testimonies*, vol. 2, p. 133; vol. 4, p. 339.
[2] Acts 16:31; *Testimonies*, vol. 5, pp. 129, 130; *The Acts of the Apostles*, p. 175.
[3] Gal. 2:20; *Testimonies*, vol. 3, p. 329.
[4] *My Life Today*, p. 340; *Temperance*, p. 150; *Testimonies*, vol. 4; p. 328; *Spiritual Gifts*, vol. 4, p. 150; *Prophets and Kings*, p. 179.
[5] *Counsels to Parents and Teachers*, p. 63; *Education*, p. 184.
[6] Rev. 2:10; *Testimonies*, vol. 2, pp. 265, 266; vol. 1, p. 74.
[7] *Counsels on Stewardship*, p. 158.
[8] Rev. 2:10, 7.
[9] Psalms 16:6; 18:19; *The Adventist Home*, p. 542; *My Life Today*, p. 350. *Counsels on Stewardship*, p. 350; *Counsels to Parents and Teachers*, p. 55.
[10] *The Great Controversy*, p. 678.
[11] *Early Writings*, p. 295.
[12] Zephaniah 3:20, *The Holy Bible: New International Version*.
[13] Rev. 22:20.